Southern Living

OUR BEST

Five-Star
RECIPES

Southern Living.

OUR BEST

Five-Star
RECIPES

Oxmoor House

ISBN: 0-8487-2788-6

Printed in the United States of America

Second Printing 2003

WE'RE HERE FOR YOU!

We at Oxmoor House are dedicated to serving you with reliable information that expands your imagination and enriches your life. We welcome your comments and suggestions.

Please write us at:

Oxmoor House, Inc.
Editor, *Southern Living*® *Our Best Five-Star Recipes*
2100 Lakeshore Drive,   Birmingham, AL 35209

To order additional publications, call 1-800-765-6400.

Editor-in-Chief: Nancy Fitzpatrick Wyatt
Senior Foods Editor: Susan Carlisle Payne
Senior Editor, Editorial Services: Olivia Kindig Wells
Art Director: James Boone

 Southern Living® *Our Best Five-Star Recipes*

Editor: Julie Fisher
Copy Editor: Keri Bradford Anderson
Associate Art Director: Cynthia R. Cooper
Senior Designer: Melissa Jones Clark
Editorial Assistant: Kaye Howard Smith
Director, Test Kitchens: Kathleen Royal Phillips
Assistant Director, Test Kitchens: Gayle Hays Sadler
Test Kitchen Home Economists: Molly Baldwin, Susan Hall Bellows, Julie Christopher, Michelle Brown Fuller,
    Natalie E. King, Elizabeth Tyler Luckett, Jan Moon, Iris Crawley O'Brien, Jan A. Smith
Senior Photographer: Jim Bathie
Senior Photo Stylist: Kay E. Clarke
Photo Stylist: Virginia R. Cravens
Additional Photography/Styling: Ralph Anderson, Colleen Duffley, Sylvia Martin, Susan Merrill,
    Beverly Morrow Perrine, Leslie Byars Simpson, E. Irene Thames, Charles E. Walton, IV, Jan Wyatt
Publishing Systems Administrator: Rick Tucker
Production and Distribution Director: Phillip Lee
Associate Production Manager: Theresa L. Beste
Production Assistant: Valerie L. Heard

Cover: *Black Forest Cake* (page 60)
Back Cover: *Spinach-Stuffed Lasagna Ruffles* (page 173)
Page 2: *Herb Garden Chicken* (page 150)

**We Want Your
FAVORITE RECIPES!**

Southern Living cooks are the best cooks of all, and we want your secrets! Please send your favorite original recipes for main dishes, desserts, and everything in between, along with any hands-on tips and a sentence about why you like each recipe. We can't guarantee we'll print them in a cookbook, but if we do, we'll send you $10 and a free copy of the cookbook. Send each recipe on a separate page with your name, address, and daytime phone number to:

Southern Living Cookbook Recipes
Oxmoor House
2100 Lakeshore Drive
Birmingham, AL 35209

Contents

Welcome

Page 17

to our new collection of the highest-rated *Southern Living* recipes with the guarantee of success. These recipes offer easy-to-find ingredients, helpful equipment lists, and pictures on every page. You'll receive accolades every time you serve them.

Page 34

★For starters, our **Texas Caviar** is an unusual and addictive black-eyed pea dip that tastes better the longer you keep it.

Page 84

★**Cloud Biscuits** rise high in the oven and will rise high on your list of easy homemade bread options.

★Our **Lemon Hearts** take the popular lemon square to a new level with heart-shaped cookie cutters and big lemon flavor.

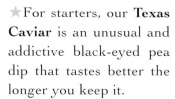

★**Texas Brunch** is a bountiful meal in itself, loaded with cheese and based on tender cornbread.

★**Little Caramel Pies** load commercial pastry crusts with a buttery caramel filling—so half the work's done for you.

Page 111

Page 122

Peek at our top pick from each chapter...

Page 152

★**Meatball Subs** are the heartiest Italian sandwiches ever to pass through our test kitchens.

★Once you put **Chicken Bundles** on the grill, the aroma of a rich molasses glaze and smoky bacon will fill the air.

Page 180

Page 198

★**Ultimate Stuffed Potatoes** overflow with cheese and bacon tucked in crispy jackets. They could easily be a one-dish meal.

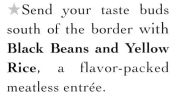

★Send your taste buds south of the border with **Black Beans and Yellow Rice**, a flavor-packed meatless entrée.

Page 225

Don't miss these memorable recipes as you flip through our "best-of-the-best" cookbook.

CUCUMBER PARTY
SANDWICHES

ROASTED GARLIC SPREAD

Appetizers & Beverages

FRONT PORCH LEMONADE

Brie with Braided Bread Ring

EQUIPMENT NEEDED:

- 8-inch round cakepan
- Baking sheet
- Pastry brush
- Wire cooling rack

Working with dough

- White bread dough is very "elastic," meaning it's stretchy, like a rubber band. Be patient as you reshape it for this recipe.

Braiding bread

- Shape bread dough into 3 long ropes; then braid them together.

Making a ring

- Wind braided dough around cakepan. Join ends of braid, firmly pinching ends to seal.

---

1 (32-ounce) package frozen white bread dough, thawed
1 tablespoon butter or margarine, melted
1 egg white, lightly beaten
1 tablespoon water
3 tablespoons sliced almonds
1 (8-inch) round fully ripened Brie, chilled
1 (12-ounce) jar strawberry or peach preserves
Garnish: strawberry fan

Combine 2 sections of dough into 1 large ball; divide into thirds. Shape each portion into a 34-inch rope on a lightly floured surface. Braid ropes together.

Invert an 8-inch round cakepan onto center of a greased baking sheet. Grease outside of cakepan. Wind braided dough around cakepan. Join ends of braid; pinch ends to seal. Brush braid with melted butter. Cover and let rise in a warm place (85°), free from drafts, 45 minutes or until doubled in bulk.

Combine egg white and water, stirring well. Brush mixture over bread, and sprinkle with almonds. Bake at 375° for 25 minutes or until golden. Carefully transfer bread ring and cakepan to a wire rack; let cool slightly. Remove cakepan from bread ring. Let bread ring cool completely.

Reduce oven temperature to 350°. Remove rind from top of Brie, leaving sides intact. Place cheese on baking sheet; top with preserves. Bake at 350° for 12 to 15 minutes or until cheese softens slightly.

Place bread ring on a serving platter. Carefully transfer cheese to center of ring. Garnish, if desired. Serve immediately. **Yield:** one 16-inch loaf.

Marinated Cheese

EQUIPMENT NEEDED:
- Glass jar with lid
- Baking dish or other shallow dish

Dressing option
- If you're in a pinch for time, forgo making the dressing for Marinated Cheese, and use an 8-ounce bottle of zesty Italian dressing instead.

Slicing cheese

- It's easiest to slice the cheeses if they're well chilled. Slice blocks of cheese in half lengthwise; then cut crosswise into ¼-inch-thick slices.

Stacking cheese

- Stand cheese slices on edge in a shallow dish, alternating types.

½ cup olive oil
½ cup white wine vinegar
3 tablespoons chopped fresh parsley
3 tablespoons minced green onions
1 teaspoon sugar
¾ teaspoon dried basil
½ teaspoon salt
½ teaspoon pepper
3 cloves garlic, minced
1 (2-ounce) jar diced pimiento, drained
1 (8-ounce) block sharp Cheddar cheese, chilled
1 (8-ounce) package cream cheese, chilled
Garnish: fresh parsley sprigs

Combine first 10 ingredients in a jar; cover tightly, and shake vigorously. Set marinade aside.

Cut block of Cheddar cheese in half lengthwise. Cut crosswise into ¼-inch-thick slices; set aside. Repeat procedure with cream cheese. Stand cheese slices on edge in a shallow dish, alternating types of cheese. Pour marinade over cheese. Cover and marinate in refrigerator at least 8 hours.

Transfer rows of marinated cheese to a serving platter in the same alternating fashion, reserving marinade. Spoon marinade over cheese slices. Garnish, if desired. Serve with assorted crackers. **Yield:** 16 appetizer servings.

Garbanzo Dip with Pita Wedges

1 (15- or 19-ounce) can garbanzo
   beans, drained
½ cup sour cream
2 tablespoons olive oil
1 tablespoon lemon juice
¼ teaspoon ground cumin
¼ teaspoon ground red pepper
2 cloves garlic, crushed

2 tablespoons sesame seeds,
   toasted
2 tablespoons chopped ripe olives
2 tablespoons minced parsley
Garnishes: sliced ripe olives,
   fresh parsley sprigs
Toasted Pita Wedges

Position knife blade in food processor bowl; add first 7 ingredients, and process until smooth. Stir in sesame seeds, chopped olives, and minced parsley. Transfer mixture to a small serving bowl. Garnish, if desired. Serve with Toasted Pita Wedges. **Yield:** 1½ cups.

Toasted Pita Wedges

1 (8-inch) white pita bread round
1 (8-inch) whole wheat pita
   bread round

2 cloves garlic, crushed
¼ cup butter or margarine,
   melted

Separate each pita bread into 2 rounds, using a sharp knife; cut each round into 6 wedges. Place on a baking sheet, smooth sides down.

  Brown garlic in melted butter in a skillet, stirring constantly. Remove from heat. Lightly brush pita wedges with garlic butter. Bake at 350° for 8 minutes or until crisp and lightly browned. **Yield:** 2 dozen.

EQUIPMENT NEEDED:
- Food processor
- Baking sheet
- Skillet
- Pastry brush

About the beans
- Garbanzo beans are also called chick-peas. They have a mild, nutty flavor.

Making pita wedges

- Separate each pita bread into 2 rounds, using a small sharp knife.

Garden Spinach Dip

1¼ cups sour cream
⅓ cup mayonnaise
¼ cup chopped green onions
1 teaspoon lemon juice
¾ teaspoon seasoned salt
¼ teaspoon dried dillweed

1 (8-ounce) can water chestnuts, drained and finely chopped
1 (10-ounce) package frozen chopped spinach, thawed and well drained
1 large purple cabbage

Combine first 7 ingredients; stir well. Add spinach, and stir well; cover and chill thoroughly.

Trim core end of cabbage to form a flat base. Cut a crosswise slice from top of cabbage, removing about one-fourth of head. Lift out enough inner leaves to form a shell about 1 inch thick (reserve slice and inner leaves of cabbage for another use). Fold back several outer leaves of cabbage, if desired.

Spoon dip into cavity of cabbage. Serve dip with assorted fresh vegetables.
Yield: 2¾ cups.

Marshmallow Fruit Dip

1 (7-ounce) jar marshmallow
    creme
½ cup mayonnaise
2 teaspoons grated orange rind
1 tablespoon orange juice

1 teaspoon grated lemon rind
1 teaspoon lemon juice
Additional grated orange and
    lemon rinds (optional)
Fresh strawberries

Combine first 6 ingredients; blend with a wire whisk until smooth.

   Spoon dip into a serving bowl; sprinkle with additional grated orange rind and lemon rind, if desired. Serve with strawberries. **Yield:** 1½ cups.

EQUIPMENT NEEDED:
- Wire whisk
- Grater

Rind before juice
- A good rule of thumb is as follows: rind before juice. It's easiest to grate rind from whole fruit; then just slice it in half to squeeze its juice.

★★★★★

EQUIPMENT NEEDED:
• Baking pan or dish
• Electric mixer

The scoop on garlic
• Don't be alarmed that this recipe uses a whole head of garlic. Garlic takes on a mellow, slightly sweet flavor as it roasts.

• Scoop out pulp (buttery soft cloves) of roasted garlic with a small spoon. Or squeeze pulp out of garlic head by hand, applying pressure at the base.

Roasted Garlic Spread

1 large head garlic	¼ cup butter, softened
1 tablespoon olive oil	½ teaspoon salt
1 (8-ounce) package cream cheese, softened	2 tablespoons minced fresh chives

Cut top off garlic, leaving head intact. Place garlic in a small baking pan; drizzle with oil. Cover with aluminum foil, and bake at 350° for 45 minutes. Uncover and bake 10 additional minutes or until garlic is soft. Remove from oven, and let cool completely. Remove and discard outermost layers of papery skin from garlic. Scoop out soft garlic pulp with a small spoon; set pulp aside.

Beat cream cheese and butter at high speed of an electric mixer until light and fluffy. Add garlic pulp and salt; beat until blended. Stir in chives. Store spread in refrigerator up to two weeks. Serve spread over warm slices of French bread. **Yield:** 1¼ cups.

Texas Caviar

1 (15½-ounce) can yellow hominy, drained
1 (15-ounce) can black-eyed peas, drained
3 green onions, finely chopped
2 cloves garlic, chopped
1 large tomato, chopped
1 medium-size green pepper, seeded and diced
1 jalapeño pepper, seeded and minced
⅓ cup chopped fresh parsley
¼ cup chopped onion
½ cup commercial zesty Italian salad dressing
Garnish: fresh parsley sprigs
Tortilla chips

Combine first 9 ingredients in a medium bowl; stir well. Pour salad dressing over black-eyed pea mixture; toss gently. Cover and chill thoroughly. Toss again before serving. Garnish, if desired. Serve with tortilla chips. **Yield:** 6½ cups.

NO SPECIAL EQUIPMENT NEEDED

Of peas and beans

• Black-eyed peas are the caviar of Texas, and they're the basis for this unusual, yet addictive, appetizer that gets better the longer it marinates.

• This recipe makes a hefty yield for a crowd. Add a 15-ounce can of black beans, drained, to make the recipe serve even more.

Chip choices

• Tortilla chips are available in many colors, depending on the type of corn used. Blue or red chips give this appetizer added flair.

Homemade Crunchy Granola

3½ cups regular oats, uncooked
½ cup grated coconut
½ cup sliced almonds
½ cup coarsely chopped pecans
½ cup wheat germ
¼ cup sesame seeds
¼ cup sunflower kernels

½ cup honey
¼ cup firmly packed brown
 sugar
¼ cup vegetable oil
½ cup crunchy peanut butter
1 teaspoon vanilla extract
¾ cup raisins (optional)

Combine first 7 ingredients in a large bowl. Stir well.

Combine honey, brown sugar, and oil in a small saucepan. Cook mixture over medium heat, stirring until sugar melts and mixture is thoroughly heated. Remove from heat; add peanut butter and vanilla, stirring until well blended. Drizzle over oat mixture; toss gently to coat well.

Spread mixture evenly in a greased 15- x 10- x 1-inch jellyroll pan. Bake at 250° for 50 to 60 minutes or until toasted and dry, stirring mixture gently every 20 minutes. Add raisins, if desired. Let granola cool completely. Store in an airtight container. **Yield:** 8 cups.

Variation: To make granola bars, press unbaked granola mixture (without raisins) into a greased 15- x 10- x 1-inch jellyroll pan, using greased fingertips. Press mixture flat with the back of a wide metal spatula. Bake at 250° for 1 hour and 20 minutes to 1½ hours or until toasted. Cut granola into bars while still warm. Let cool completely in pan. Remove bars from pan, and store in an airtight container. **Yield:** 30 bars.

EQUIPMENT NEEDED:
• Saucepan
• Jellyroll pan
• Metal spatula

Breakfast options
• This granola is also good sprinkled over pancakes or waffles, or stirred into pancake batter.

Granola bars

• If you make granola bars, cut the bars while granola is warm, but wait until bars completely cool before removing them from the pan. This helps them come out of the pan and hold their shape.

EQUIPMENT NEEDED:

- Food processor
- 2½-inch round cutter
- Decorating bag with No. 4 tip or heavy-duty, zip-top plastic bag

Zip-top option

- You don't have to own piping tips for this recipe. Just spoon filling into a zip-top plastic bag, seal, and snip a tiny hole in a corner. Squeeze mixture onto each sandwich.

Filling the food chute

- Spoon vegetable mixture through food chute while processor is running.

Cutting bread rounds

- Cut bread into rounds with a 2½-inch cutter. Crumble remaining bread trimmings for a stuffing.

Cucumber Party Sandwiches

1 medium onion, quartered
1 large cucumber, peeled, seeded, and cut into chunks
2 (8-ounce) packages cream cheese, softened
½ teaspoon salt
⅛ teaspoon ground white pepper
40 (¼-inch-thick) slices white bread
40 (¼-inch-thick) slices whole wheat bread
1 (8-ounce) package cream cheese, softened
1 tablespoon milk
2 teaspoons minced fresh dillweed
Garnishes: cucumber slices, radish slices, dillweed sprigs

Position knife blade in food processor bowl; add onion and cucumber chunks. Process 8 to 10 seconds or until vegetables are finely chopped, scraping sides of processor bowl once. Drain well on paper towels.

Position plastic blade in food processor bowl. Cut 2 packages of cream cheese into 1-inch pieces; place in processor bowl. Process 8 to 10 seconds or until smooth. Spoon vegetable mixture, salt, and pepper through food chute with processor running; process mixture 25 to 30 seconds or until blended, scraping sides of processor bowl once. Cover and chill.

Cut white bread slices into 40 rounds with a 2½-inch round cutter. Repeat procedure with wheat bread. Reserve remaining bread trimmings for another use.

Spread 1 tablespoon cheese mixture on 1 side of each white bread round; top each with a wheat bread round. Turn half of sandwiches wheat bread side up.

Combine 1 package cream cheese, milk, and minced dillweed in food processor bowl; process until smooth. Spoon mixture into a decorating bag fitted with metal tip No. 4. Pipe a rosette of cream cheese mixture on each sandwich. Garnish each sandwich with cucumber or radish slices and dillweed sprigs, if desired. **Yield:** 40 appetizers.

Spicy Chicken Strips

8 skinned and boned chicken
   breast halves
¾ cup all-purpose flour
1½ teaspoons chili powder
¾ teaspoon salt
½ teaspoon garlic powder

¼ teaspoon ground cumin
¼ teaspoon pepper
1 large egg, lightly beaten
½ cup water
Vegetable oil
Tomato-Garlic Dip

Cut chicken into long, thin strips (about ¾ inch wide).

  Combine flour and next 5 ingredients; stir well. Stir in egg and water. Dip chicken strips in batter.

  Fry strips, a few at a time, in hot oil (375°) for 2 to 3 minutes or until golden. Drain on paper towels. Serve immediately with Tomato-Garlic Dip. **Yield:** 16 appetizer servings.

Tomato-Garlic Dip

⅓ cup mayonnaise
¼ cup sour cream
¼ cup tomato sauce
¼ teaspoon ground cumin

¼ teaspoon chili powder
¼ teaspoon hot sauce
2 cloves garlic, crushed
1 (6-ounce) can tomato paste

Combine all ingredients in a small bowl; stir well. Serve dip in a hollowed out cabbage bowl, if desired. (See page 14 for cabbage bowl directions.) **Yield:** 1½ cups.

Chicken strips

• Cut chicken into long, thin strips. Depending on the size, you can probably cut 4 strips from each breast half.

On frying

• Fry coated chicken strips, a few at a time, lowering them into the hot oil with a long-handled spoon to protect from spattering.

Egg Rolls

Wrap and roll

- Fold 3 corners of each egg roll wrapper over filling as recipe directs; then brush remaining corner of wrapper with egg mixture. This helps the roll stick together during frying.

Freezing Egg Rolls

- To freeze Egg Rolls, fry them as directed, and let cool. Wrap in aluminum foil. Place in zip-top plastic bags, and freeze up to one month. To serve, uncover and bake at 425° for 15 to 20 minutes or until thoroughly heated.

1½ teaspoons cornstarch
¼ cup soy sauce, divided
2 tablespoons grated fresh ginger, divided
1 clove garlic, crushed
½ pound lean boneless pork, diced
1½ pounds unpeeled small fresh shrimp, peeled and coarsely chopped
1 tablespoon rice wine
2 tablespoons peanut oil
5 cups shredded cabbage
½ cup diced onion
½ cup diced celery
3 medium carrots, scraped and shredded
½ cup bean sprouts, chopped
1 (8-ounce) can bamboo shoots, drained and chopped
(8-ounce) can water chestnuts, drained and chopped
½ teaspoon dry mustard
1 large egg, lightly beaten
2 teaspoons water
2 (1-pound) packages egg roll wrappers
Additional peanut oil
Sweet-and-sour sauce (optional)
Hot mustard sauce (optional)

Combine cornstarch, 2 tablespoons soy sauce, 1 tablespoon ginger, and garlic; stir well. Stir in pork; let stand 15 minutes. Combine shrimp and rice wine; let stand 15 minutes. Heat 2 tablespoons oil in a preheated wok or large nonstick skillet, coating sides; heat at medium-high (375°) 2 minutes. Add pork and shrimp mixtures; stir-fry 2 to 3 minutes or until pork and shrimp are cooked. Remove from wok. Cover; keep warm.

Add cabbage, onion, and celery to wok; stir-fry 2 to 3 minutes or until crisp-tender. Add carrot and next 3 ingredients; stir-fry 2 minutes. Add pork and shrimp, stirring well. Combine remaining 2 tablespoons soy sauce, remaining 1 tablespoon ginger, and mustard; stir well, and add to wok. Stir-fry 1 minute. Remove mixture from wok.

Combine egg and water; stir well. Mound ⅓ cup filling in center of each egg roll wrapper. Fold 1 corner of wrapper over filling; then fold top and bottom corners over filling. Push filling toward center. Lightly brush remaining corner of wrapper with egg mixture. Tightly roll filled end toward exposed corner, and gently press corner to seal securely.

Pour additional oil into wok to depth of 1½ inches. Heat to 375°. Place 2 egg rolls in hot oil; fry 35 to 45 seconds on each side or until golden; drain on paper towels. Repeat with remaining egg rolls. If desired, serve with sweet-and-sour sauce and hot mustard sauce. **Yield:** 2 dozen.

Dill Pickle Chips

2 pints sliced dill pickles, undrained
1 large egg, lightly beaten
1 tablespoon all-purpose flour
½ teaspoon hot sauce

1½ cups all-purpose flour
2½ teaspoons ground red pepper
1 teaspoon garlic powder
¼ teaspoon salt
Vegetable oil

Drain pickles, reserving ⅔ cup pickle juice. Press pickles between paper towels to remove excess moisture. Combine ⅔ cup pickle juice, egg, 1 tablespoon flour, and hot sauce; stir well, and set aside.

Combine 1½ cups flour and next 3 ingredients; stir well. Dip pickles in egg mixture; dredge in flour mixture.

Pour oil to depth of 1½ inches if using a skillet. Fry coated pickles, in batches, in hot oil (375°) for 2 to 3 minutes or until golden, turning once. Drain on paper towels. Serve immediately. **Yield:** about 10½ dozen.

EQUIPMENT NEEDED:

• Large glass bowl
• Saucepan
• 7 pint jars with lids
• Metal funnel
• Ladle or large serving spoon
• Tongs
• Kettle or Dutch oven

Squash math

• Five pounds of yellow squash should measure about 16 cups once you slice it.

Ladling squash

• Pack vegetables into hot sterilized jars. A ladle and funnel keep the task neat.

Sealing jars

• Process pickles in boiling-water bath. You'll know the jar lids have sealed when you hear the lids pop.

Squash Pickles

16 cups sliced small yellow squash (about 5 pounds)
2 large onions, sliced
½ cup salt
1 (4-ounce) jar sliced pimiento, drained
3½ cups sugar

2¼ cups white vinegar (5% acidity)
2 tablespoons plus 1 teaspoon pickling salt
1 tablespoon celery seeds
1 tablespoon mustard seeds
1½ teaspoons ground turmeric

Combine squash and onion in a large glass bowl; sprinkle with ½ cup salt. Cover and let stand 2 hours. Rinse vegetables several times in cold water; drain well. Add pimiento to vegetable mixture.

Combine sugar and remaining 5 ingredients in a saucepan; bring to a boil. Cook until sugar dissolves, stirring often.

Pack vegetables into hot sterilized pint jars; cover with hot syrup, filling to ½ inch from top. Remove air bubbles; wipe jar rims. Cover at once with metal lids, and screw on bands. Process in boiling-water bath 15 minutes. **Yield:** *7 pints.*

Blender Strawberry Daiquiris

EQUIPMENT NEEDED:
• Electric blender

Slushy berries

• Partially thaw frozen strawberries easily by dipping them (still in the bag) in hot water about 30 seconds; then remove bag from water, and add "slushy" berries to the blender.

1 (10-ounce) package frozen strawberries in light syrup, partially thawed
½ (12-ounce) can frozen pink lemonade concentrate, thawed and undiluted
¾ cup light rum
2 tablespoons powdered sugar
3½ cups crushed ice
Garnish: fresh strawberries

Combine partially thawed strawberries and next 3 ingredients in container of an electric blender. Cover; process just until blended. Add crushed ice; cover and process just until smooth. Garnish each serving, if desired. Serve immediately. **Yield:** 5 cups.

EQUIPMENT NEEDED:
• Two ice cube trays

Edible flowers
• Pansies and nasturtiums are edible flowers that provide vivid color for dressed-up ice cubes. Use flowers that haven't been treated with pesticides.

Colorful cubes

• Use boiling water to make the clearest ice cubes. Regular tap water looks cloudy after freezing, so the vibrant flowers would not display as well.

Front Porch Lemonade

1¼ cups sugar
½ cup boiling water
4½ cups cold water

1½ cups fresh lemon juice (about 12 lemons)
28 edible flowers

Combine sugar and boiling water, stirring until sugar dissolves. Add cold water and lemon juice; stir well. Chill thoroughly.

   Place 1 flower in each compartment of two ice cube trays. Boil enough water to fill trays; let cool completely. Fill trays with cooled water; freeze. Serve lemonade over ice cubes. **Yield:** *7 cups.*

Preparing ice mold

• Lightly spray the ring mold with cooking spray to help ice ring slip easily out of the mold once it's frozen.

• Arrange orange slices, lime slices, and cherries in mold once it's frozen to a slushy appearance. This way, the fruit will stay suspended in the liquid.

Basic Party Punch

Vegetable cooking spray	2 quarts boiling water
3¾ cups orange juice, divided	5 cups sugar
4 to 6 orange slices	5 quarts cold water
4 to 6 lime slices	1 (46-ounce) can pineapple juice, chilled
4 to 6 maraschino cherries with stems	1 (6-ounce) can frozen orange juice concentrate, thawed and undiluted
¼ cup citric acid or ascorbic citric powder	

Lightly spray a 4½-cup ring mold with cooking spray. Pour 3 cups orange juice into mold; freeze until slushy. Arrange orange slices, lime slices, and cherries in mold. Fill mold with remaining ¾ cup orange juice, and freeze until firm.

Combine citric acid and boiling water in a large nonmetal container; stir until citric acid dissolves. Cover; let stand at room temperature 24 hours.

Combine sugar and cold water in a large nonmetal container; stir until sugar dissolves. Add citric acid mixture, pineapple juice, and orange juice concentrate; stir punch well.

Remove ice ring from freezer; let stand at room temperature 2 to 3 minutes; unmold ice ring into bottom of a punch bowl. Gently pour punch over ice ring in punch bowl. **Yield:** 2 gallons.

Coffee-Kahlúa Punch

6 cups hot brewed coffee
2 cups milk
½ cup sugar
1 tablespoon vanilla extract
2 cups Kahlúa or other
   coffee-flavored liqueur

1 quart vanilla ice cream
1 quart coffee ice cream
Garnish: shaved semisweet
   chocolate

Combine first 4 ingredients in a large bowl; stir until sugar dissolves. Chill thoroughly.

  Pour chilled coffee mixture and Kahlúa into a punch bowl, stirring gently. Scoop ice creams into punch bowl. Garnish, if desired. **Yield:** 4½ quarts.

EQUIPMENT NEEDED:
- Punch bowl
- Ice cream scoop or large spoon
- Vegetable peeler

Chocolate shavings

- This rich punch will please a big crowd. Place a small dish of chocolate shavings near the punch so that each guest can sprinkle chocolate in their punch cup.

- It's easy to make chocolate shavings if you use a vegetable peeler and a firm piece of chocolate. Work quickly, because the warmth of your hand will melt the chocolate if you hold it too long.

Wassail

4 (3-inch) sticks cinnamon,
 broken
1 teaspoon whole cloves
3 quarts apple cider
1 cup apricot nectar
⅔ cup firmly packed brown
 sugar
1 teaspoon ground allspice
½ teaspoon ground ginger
½ teaspoon ground cinnamon

1 (6-ounce) can frozen lemonade
 concentrate, thawed and
 undiluted
1 (6-ounce) can frozen orange
 juice concentrate, thawed
 and undiluted
1 (12-ounce) can beer (optional)
Garnishes: apple slices, orange
 slices and wedges, whole
 cloves

EQUIPMENT NEEDED:
• Cheesecloth
• Dutch oven

What's Wassail?
• Wassail is a hot spiced drink (like cider) that contains ale or wine. Our version gives you the option to add beer; however, Wassail is every bit as good without alcohol.

Tie cinnamon sticks and 1 teaspoon cloves in a cheesecloth bag. Combine spice bag, cider, and next 7 ingredients in a Dutch oven. Bring to a boil; reduce heat, and simmer, uncovered, 20 minutes.

Add beer, if desired, and simmer until ready to serve. Discard spice bag. Garnish with fruit slices studded with whole cloves, if desired. **Yield:** 16 cups.

TOASTED PECAN WAFFLES

GLAZED
DOUGHNUTS

Breads

BUTTERY
PAN ROLLS

Cloud Biscuits

EQUIPMENT NEEDED:
- Pastry blender or two knives
- Rolling pin
- 3-inch biscuit cutter
- Baking sheet
- Small pastry brush

Cutting in shortening

- Cut butter-flavored shortening into flour mixture with a pastry blender. If you don't have a pastry blender, you can cut back and forth through the mixture with two knives.

Rolling dough
- When you're rolling out biscuit dough, keep the pressure on the rolling pin light so the biscuits will rise high.

Punch, don't twist
- Use a metal biscuit cutter dipped in flour to punch out biscuits in a quick motion. Don't twist the cutter, or you'll seal the edges and the biscuits won't rise.

2¼ cups self-rising flour
1 tablespoon sugar
½ cup butter-flavored shortening
1 large egg, lightly beaten

⅔ cup milk
1 tablespoon butter or margarine, melted

Combine flour and sugar in a medium bowl; stir well. Cut in shortening with a pastry blender until mixture is crumbly.

Combine egg and milk; add to flour mixture, stirring just until dry ingredients are moistened. Turn dough out onto a floured surface, and knead 3 or 4 times.

Roll dough to ½-inch thickness; cut with a 3-inch biscuit cutter. Place biscuits on an ungreased baking sheet. Bake at 450° for 10 to 12 minutes or until golden. Remove from oven; brush hot biscuits with melted butter. **Yield:** 1 dozen.

Breakfast Scones

2 cups all-purpose flour	½ cup sour cream
2 teaspoons baking powder	1 large egg, lightly beaten
½ teaspoon baking soda	⅔ cup currants (optional)
¼ teaspoon salt	2 teaspoons milk
3 tablespoons sugar	1 tablespoon sugar
⅓ cup butter or margarine	Strawberry Butter

Combine first 5 ingredients in a medium bowl; stir well. Cut in butter with a pastry blender until mixture is crumbly.

  Add sour cream and egg, stirring just until dry ingredients are moistened. Stir in currants, if desired.

  Turn dough out onto a lightly floured surface, and knead lightly 4 or 5 times. Pat dough to an 8-inch circle on a greased baking sheet. Brush top with milk; sprinkle with 1 tablespoon sugar. Cut circle into 8 wedges, using a sharp knife; separate wedges slightly. Bake at 400° for 14 to 16 minutes or until lightly browned. Serve scones warm with Strawberry Butter. **Yield:** 8 scones.

Strawberry Butter

½ cup butter, softened	2½ tablespoons strawberry preserves

Beat butter at medium speed of an electric mixer until creamy, or beat vigorously with a wooden spoon. Stir in preserves. Transfer mixture to a serving bowl. **Yield:** ½ cup.

EQUIPMENT NEEDED:
- Pastry blender or two knives
- Baking sheet
- Small pastry brush
- Electric mixer or wooden spoon

Patting into shape

- Pat dough into an 8-inch circle on baking sheet. Scones will bake lighter and higher if you pat rather than roll dough into shape.

Sugar coating

- Brush top of dough with milk; then sprinkle with sugar. This bakes into a crusty sweet topping.

Herbed Jumbo Popovers

EQUIPMENT NEEDED:

- Popover pan or large custard cups
- Wire whisk

About flour

• Bread flour is the key ingredient that gives these popovers a sturdy structure as they bake and rise high out of the pan. You can substitute all-purpose flour, but the popovers may not be quite as jumbo.

Preparing pan

• Heavily grease popover pan, and dust bottom and sides with cheese. Cheese helps the popover batter climb the sides of the pan as it puffs and bakes.

Vegetable cooking spray or vegetable oil
2 tablespoons grated Parmesan cheese
1 cup bread flour
1 cup milk
1 tablespoon butter or margarine, melted

1 teaspoon dried thyme
1 teaspoon Worcestershire sauce
¾ teaspoon dried oregano
½ teaspoon salt
¼ teaspoon garlic powder
2 large eggs, lightly beaten
2 egg whites

Heavily grease a popover pan with cooking spray or oil, and dust bottom and sides of pan with Parmesan cheese. Set pan aside.

Combine flour and remaining ingredients; stir mixture with a wire whisk until blended. Fill prepared pan three-fourths full. Place in a cold oven. Turn oven to 450°, and bake 15 minutes. Reduce heat to 350°, and bake 35 to 40 additional minutes or until popovers are crusty and brown. Serve immediately. **Yield:** 6 popovers.

Lemon Tea Bread

1 (8-ounce) package cream
   cheese, softened
½ cup butter or margarine,
   softened
1¼ cups sugar
2 large eggs
2¼ cups all-purpose flour
1 tablespoon baking powder

½ teaspoon salt
¾ cup milk
1 tablespoon grated lemon rind,
   divided
⅔ cup finely chopped blanched
   almonds, toasted
⅔ cup sifted powdered sugar
2 tablespoons lemon juice

Beat cream cheese and butter at high speed of an electric mixer until light and fluffy. Gradually add 1¼ cups sugar, beating well. Add eggs, one at a time, beating well after each addition.

Combine flour, baking powder, and salt; add to creamed mixture alternately with milk, beginning and ending with flour mixture. Mix after each addition. Stir in 2 teaspoons lemon rind and almonds. Pour batter into two greased and floured 8½- x 4½- x 3-inch loafpans.

Bake at 350° for 45 minutes or until a wooden pick inserted in center comes out clean.

Combine remaining 1 teaspoon lemon rind, powdered sugar, and lemon juice, stirring well. Spoon glaze over warm loaves. Let cool in pans 10 minutes. Remove from pans, and cool completely on a wire rack. **Yield:** 2 loaves.

EQUIPMENT NEEDED:
- Electric mixer
- Two 8½ - x 4½ - x 3-inch loafpans
- Wire cooling rack

Glazing

- Spoon glaze over loaves while they're warm. This lets the glaze soak in and keeps the loaves very moist.

EQUIPMENT NEEDED:
- Electric mixer
- 9- x 5- x 3-inch loafpan
- Wire cooling rack

Banana basics

- Ripe bananas mash easily with a fork. Speed up the ripening process of firm bananas by placing them in a brown paper sack for a day.

Variations:
- **Banana-Nut Muffins:** Spoon batter into greased muffin pans, filling three-fourths full. Sprinkle tops with 1 tablespoon wheat germ. Bake at 400° for 20 to 22 minutes. Remove muffins from pans immediately. **Yield:** 1½ dozen.

- **Chocolate Chip-Banana-Nut Bread:** Stir ¾ cup chocolate mini-morsels into batter before baking.

Banana-Nut Bread

½ cup butter or margarine, softened
¾ cup firmly packed brown sugar
2 large eggs
2 cups all-purpose flour
1½ teaspoons baking powder
½ teaspoon baking soda
½ teaspoon salt
¼ cup wheat germ
½ teaspoon ground cinnamon
3 large ripe bananas, mashed
1½ teaspoons instant coffee granules
2 tablespoons hot water
⅔ cup chopped pecans
1 teaspoon vanilla extract
1 tablespoon wheat germ

Beat butter at medium speed of an electric mixer until creamy; gradually add sugar, beating well. Add eggs, one at a time, beating well.

Combine flour and next 5 ingredients; stir well. Add to creamed mixture alternately with mashed banana, beginning and ending with dry ingredients. Dissolve coffee granules in hot water. Stir into batter. Stir in pecans and vanilla.

Spoon batter evenly into a greased and lightly floured 9- x 5- x 3-inch loafpan. Sprinkle with 1 tablespoon wheat germ. Bake at 350° for 1 hour or until a wooden pick inserted in center comes out clean. Let cool in pan 10 minutes. Remove from pan, and let cool on a wire rack. **Yield:** 1 loaf.

Toasted Pecan Waffles

3¼ cups all-purpose flour
1 tablespoon baking powder
½ teaspoon baking soda
1 teaspoon salt
3 tablespoons sugar
3 cups chopped pecans, toasted
4 cups buttermilk

¾ cup butter or margarine,
   melted
4 large eggs, separated
Butter curls (optional)
Syrup (optional)
Toasted pecan halves (optional)

Combine first 5 ingredients in a large mixing bowl; stir well. Stir in chopped pecans. Combine buttermilk, melted butter, and egg yolks; stir well. Add to flour mixture, stirring just until dry ingredients are moistened.

Beat egg whites at high speed of an electric mixer until stiff peaks form; carefully fold beaten egg whites into batter.

Pour 1 cup batter into a preheated, oiled waffle iron. Cook about 5 minutes or until golden. Repeat procedure with remaining batter. If desired, serve waffles with butter curls, syrup, and pecan halves. **Yield:** 36 (4-inch) waffles.

Note: To freeze waffles, cook as directed; let cool. Wrap in aluminum foil, and freeze. To serve, reheat in toaster.

EQUIPMENT NEEDED:

• Electric mixer
• Waffle iron
• Pastry brush
• Butter curler (optional)

Oiling waffle iron

• Brush waffle iron with oil. This prevents batter from sticking in the grooves.

Curling butter

• For fancy butter curls, pull a butter curler across a stick of cold butter. Keep curls in ice water until ready to use.

Zucchini Bread with Cheese Spread

EQUIPMENT NEEDED:
- 12 miniature Bundt pans or two 8½- x 4½- x 3-inch loafpans
- Grater
- Wire cooling racks
- Electric mixer

Preparing zucchini

- Press zucchini between paper towels to soak up excess moisture so bread won't be soggy.

3 cups all-purpose flour
1 teaspoon baking soda
¾ teaspoon salt
1½ teaspoons ground cinnamon
¼ teaspoon ground cloves
⅛ teaspoon ground ginger
⅛ teaspoon ground nutmeg
1 cup chopped walnuts or pecans
¾ cup chopped dates

2 cups coarsely shredded zucchini
1 cup sugar
¾ cup firmly packed brown sugar
1 cup vegetable oil
¼ cup plus 2 tablespoons milk
2 teaspoons vanilla extract
3 large eggs, lightly beaten
Cheese Spread

Combine first 7 ingredients; stir in walnuts and dates.

Press zucchini between paper towels to remove excess moisture. Combine zucchini, 1 cup sugar, and next 5 ingredients; stir well. Add zucchini mixture to flour mixture, stirring just until dry ingredients are moistened.

Pour batter into 12 greased and floured 1-cup miniature Bundt pans. Bake at 350° for 25 to 35 minutes or until a wooden pick inserted in center comes out clean. Let cool in pans 5 minutes. Remove from pans, and let cool on wire racks. Serve with Cheese Spread. **Yield:** 12 (4-inch) loaves.

Cheese Spread

1 (8-ounce) package cream cheese, softened
1½ tablespoons powdered sugar
1 tablespoon pineapple juice
½ teaspoon vanilla extract

3 tablespoons drained crushed pineapple
2 tablespoons finely chopped walnuts or pecans

Combine first 4 ingredients in a small mixing bowl; beat at medium speed of an electric mixer until smooth. Add pineapple and walnuts, stirring well. Store spread in the refrigerator. **Yield:** 1¼ cups.

Note: Bake Zucchini Bread in two greased and floured 8½- x 4½- x 3-inch loafpans, if desired. Bake at 350° for 1 hour or until a wooden pick inserted in center of loaves comes out clean.

EQUIPMENT NEEDED:
- Thermometer for yeast
- Electric mixer
- Two 9-inch square pans
- Small pastry brush

Letting dough rise

- Let the dough rise in an oven with a pan of hot water. This provides a draft-free environment and the ideal rising temperature (85°).

Shaping rolls

- Pinch off small balls of dough, and shape them into 1½-inch balls. Dip in melted butter.

Buttery Pan Rolls

5½ cups all-purpose flour, divided	1½ cups milk
3 tablespoons sugar	½ cup water
2 teaspoons salt	½ cup plus 2 tablespoons butter or margarine, divided
1 package active dry yeast	

Combine 3 cups flour and next 3 ingredients a large bowl; stir well.

Combine milk, water, and ¼ cup butter in a saucepan; cook mixture over medium heat until butter melts, stirring occasionally. Remove from heat, and let cool to 120° to 130°.

Gradually add milk mixture to flour mixture, beating at low speed of an electric mixer 30 seconds. Beat at high speed 2 minutes. Gradually stir in enough of remaining 2½ cups flour to make a soft dough.

Turn dough out onto a lightly floured surface, and knead until smooth and elastic (8 to 10 minutes). Place dough in a well-greased bowl, turning to grease top. Cover and let rise in a warm place (85°), free from drafts, 1 hour and 15 minutes or until doubled in bulk.

Punch dough down; cover and let rest 10 minutes. Melt remaining ¼ cup plus 2 tablespoons butter.

Pinch off small balls of dough, and shape into 40 (1½-inch) balls; dip each ball in melted butter. Place balls in two greased 9-inch square baking pans. Cover and let rise in a warm place, free from drafts, 45 minutes or until doubled in bulk. Bake at 375° for 15 minutes or until rolls are golden. Brush warm rolls with any remaining melted butter. **Yield:** 40 rolls.

Whole Wheat-Buttermilk Bread

1 package active dry yeast
2 tablespoons sugar
½ cup warm water (105° to 115°)
1 cup buttermilk
¼ cup vegetable oil

3 tablespoons honey
1 large egg, lightly beaten
1¾ cups whole wheat flour
1 teaspoon salt
⅛ teaspoon baking powder
2¼ to 2¾ cups bread flour

Dissolve yeast and sugar in warm water in a large bowl; let stand 5 minutes. Add buttermilk and next 3 ingredients, stirring well. Add whole wheat flour, salt, and baking powder; beat at medium speed of an electric mixer 3 minutes or until smooth. Gradually stir in enough bread flour to make a soft dough.

Turn dough out onto a floured surface, and knead until smooth and elastic (about 8 to 10 minutes). Place dough in a well-greased bowl, turning to grease top. Cover and let rise in a warm place (85°), free from drafts, 1½ hours or until doubled in bulk.

Punch dough down, and divide in half. Roll each half into a 15- x 8-inch rectangle. Roll dough, jellyroll fashion, starting with narrow end; pinch seams and ends to seal. Place loaves, seam side down, in two greased 8½- x 4½- x 3-inch loafpans. Cover and let rise in a warm place, free from drafts, 1 hour or until doubled in bulk. Bake at 350° for 30 minutes or until loaves sound hollow when tapped. Cover with aluminum foil the last 10 minutes of baking to prevent excessive browning, if necessary. Remove loaves from pans, and let cool on a wire rack. **Yield:** 2 loaves.

EQUIPMENT NEEDED:
• Thermometer for yeast
• Electric mixer
• Two 8½- x 4½- x 3-inch loafpans
• Wire cooling rack

Water temperature

• A thermometer helps you detect the proper temperature (105° to 115°) for the water. Water that's too hot will kill the yeast, while water that's too cool will slow the dough's rising.

Homemade Sourdough Bread

EQUIPMENT NEEDED:
- Thermometer for yeast
- Electric mixer
- Rolling pin
- Two 9- x 5- x 3-inch loafpans
- Pastry brush
- Wire cooling rack

Sourdough sense
- Create this crusty bread with tangy flavor by using a sourdough yeast starter as leavening. Keep feeding Starter Food, and you can use it indefinitely.

2 packages active dry yeast
1¼ cups warm water (105° to 115°)
1 cup Sourdough Starter (at room temperature)
¼ cup vegetable oil
¼ cup sugar
2 teaspoons salt
2 large eggs, lightly beaten
6 to 7 cups unbleached all-purpose flour, divided
Additional vegetable oil
Butter or margarine, melted

Dissolve yeast in warm water in a large nonmetal bowl; let stand 5 minutes. Add 1 cup Sourdough Starter and next 4 ingredients, stirring well to combine. Add 3 cups flour; beat at medium speed of an electric mixer until blended. Gradually stir in enough of remaining 4 cups flour to make a soft dough. Turn dough out onto a well-floured surface, and knead until smooth and elastic (about 5 minutes). Place in a well-greased bowl, turning to grease top. Cover and let rise in a warm place (85°), free from drafts, 1 hour or until dough is doubled in bulk.

Punch dough down; turn out onto a lightly floured surface, and knead lightly 4 or 5 times. Divide in half. Roll half of dough to a 14- x 7-inch rectangle. Roll up dough, starting at short side, pressing firmly to eliminate air pockets; pinch ends to seal. Place, seam side down, in a well-greased 9- x 5- x 3-inch loafpan. Repeat procedure with remaining dough.

Cover and let rise in a warm place, free from drafts, 45 minutes or until doubled in bulk. Brush tops of loaves with additional oil. Bake at 375° for 30 to 35 minutes or until loaves sound hollow when tapped. Remove bread from pans; brush with melted butter. Let cool on a wire rack. **Yield:** 2 loaves.

Sourdough Starter

1 package active dry yeast
½ cup warm water (105° to 115°)
2 cups all-purpose flour
3 tablespoons sugar
1 teaspoon salt
2 cups warm water (105° to 115°)
Starter Food (facing page)

Dissolve yeast in ½ cup warm water; let stand 5 minutes. Combine flour, sugar, and salt in a nonmetal bowl. Gradually stir in 2 cups warm water. Stir in yeast mixture. Cover loosely with plastic wrap; let stand in a warm place (85°) for 72 hours, stirring three times daily. Place in refrigerator; stir once a day. (Use starter within 11 days.)

To use, remove starter from refrigerator; let stand at room temperature at least 1 hour. Stir well; measure amount needed for recipe. Add Starter Food after each use to replenish remaining starter. Place in refrigerator; stir once a day. (Use again within 2 to 14 days.) **Yield:** 3 cups.

Starter Food

1 cup all-purpose flour **1 cup milk**
½ cup sugar

Add all ingredients to remaining Sourdough Starter, stirring well.

Cream Cheese Rolls

EQUIPMENT NEEDED:

- Saucepan
- Thermometer for yeast
- Rolling pin
- Unwaxed dental floss or sharp knife
- Baking sheet
- Wire cooling rack
- Electric mixer

Cutting dough

- To cut roll of dough, slip dental floss or strong thread under roll, and crisscross over top of roll, pulling floss to cut dough. Or, you can use a sharp knife.

1 (8-ounce) carton sour cream
½ cup sugar
½ cup butter or margarine
1 teaspoon salt
2 packages active dry yeast
½ cup warm water (105° to 115°)
2 large eggs, lightly beaten
4 to 5 cups all-purpose flour
Filling
Glaze

Combine first 4 ingredients in a saucepan. Cook over medium heat until butter melts, stirring occasionally. Let cool to 105° to 115°.

Dissolve yeast in warm water in a large bowl; let stand 5 minutes. Stir in sour cream mixture and eggs. Gradually stir in enough flour to make a soft dough (dough will be sticky). Cover tightly, and chill 8 hours.

Divide dough into 4 equal portions. Working with 1 portion at a time, turn dough out onto a floured surface; knead 4 or 5 times. Roll 1 portion of dough to a 12- x 8-inch rectangle. Spread one-fourth of Filling over rectangle, leaving a ½-inch margin around edges. Carefully roll up dough, jellyroll fashion, beginning at long side. Firmly pinch seam to seal. Cut roll into 1-inch slices; place slices 2 inches apart on a greased baking sheet. Repeat procedure with remaining dough and Filling.

Cover and let rise in a warm place (85°), free from drafts, 45 minutes to 1 hour or until doubled in bulk. Bake at 375° for 15 to 20 minutes or until rolls are lightly browned. Remove rolls to wire racks, and drizzle Glaze over warm rolls. **Yield:** 4 dozen.

Filling

2 (8-ounce) packages cream cheese, softened
¾ cup sugar
2 teaspoons vanilla extract
⅛ teaspoon salt
1 large egg

Combine all ingredients in a large bowl. Beat at high speed of an electric mixer until blended. **Yield:** 2½ cups.

Glaze

2 cups sifted powdered sugar
¼ cup milk
2 teaspoons vanilla extract

Combine all ingredients in a bowl, stirring until smooth. **Yield:** ¾ cup.

Beignets

1 package active dry yeast
3 tablespoons warm water (105°
   to 115°)
¾ cup milk
¼ cup sugar
¼ cup shortening

1 teaspoon salt
3 cups all-purpose flour, divided
1 large egg
Vegetable oil
Powdered sugar

Dissolve yeast in warm water in a large bowl; let stand 5 minutes.

   Combine milk and next 3 ingredients in a saucepan; cook over low heat until shortening melts, stirring occasionally. Let cool to 105° to 115°. Add milk mixture, 2 cups flour, and egg to yeast mixture; beat at medium speed of an electric mixer 2 minutes. Gradually stir in enough of remaining 1 cup flour to make a soft dough.

   Turn dough out onto a lightly floured surface, and knead until smooth and elastic (8 to 10 minutes). Place in a well-greased bowl, turning to grease top. Cover and let rise in a warm place (85°), free from drafts, 1 hour or until dough is doubled in bulk.

   Punch dough down; turn out onto a floured surface. Roll dough into a 12- x 10-inch rectangle, and cut into 2-inch squares. Place squares on a lightly floured surface; cover and let rise in a warm place, free from drafts, 45 minutes or until doubled in bulk.

   Pour oil to a depth of 3 to 4 inches into a large heavy skillet; heat oil to 375°. Fry beignets in hot oil, three or four at a time, 1 minute on each side or until golden. Drain beignets on paper towels, and sprinkle with powdered sugar. **Yield:** 2½ dozen.

EQUIPMENT NEEDED:
- Saucepan
- Thermometer for yeast
- Electric mixer
- Rolling pin
- Large heavy skillet
- Clip-on thermometer
- Sifter or tea strainer

Letting dough rise

• Place dough in a well-greased bowl, turning it to grease the top. This will prevent dough from drying out while it rises.

Frying beignets

• Fry beignets in hot oil, three or four at a time, 1 minute on each side or until golden. If you fry too many beignets at once, the oil will cool down.

Glazed Doughnuts

1 package active dry yeast	½ teaspoon salt
2 tablespoons warm water (105° to 115°)	½ teaspoon ground nutmeg
¾ cup warm milk (105° to 115°)	⅛ teaspoon ground cinnamon
2½ cups bread flour, divided	1 large egg
¼ cup sugar	Vegetable oil
3 tablespoons shortening	White Glaze
	Chocolate Glaze

Dissolve yeast in warm water in a large mixing bowl. Let stand 5 minutes. Add milk, 1 cup flour, and next 6 ingredients; beat mixture at medium speed of an electric mixer 2 minutes or until blended. Stir in remaining 1½ cups flour. Cover and let rise in a warm place (85°), free from drafts, 1 hour or until doubled in bulk.

Punch dough down; turn out onto a well-floured surface, and knead until smooth and elastic. Roll dough to ½-inch thickness, and cut with a 2½-inch doughnut cutter. Place doughnuts on a lightly floured surface. Cover and let rise in a warm place, free from drafts, 20 to 30 minutes or until doubled in bulk.

Pour oil to a depth of 2 to 3 inches into a Dutch oven. Heat to 375°; drop in 4 or 5 doughnuts at a time. Cook 1 minute or until golden on 1 side; turn and cook other side until golden. Drain well. Dip each doughnut into White Glaze or Chocolate Glaze while warm, and place on wire racks, letting excess glaze drip off. **Yield:** 1 dozen.

White Glaze

2 cups sifted powdered sugar	3 tablespoons milk

Combine powdered sugar and milk in a bowl, stirring until mixture is smooth. **Yield:** ¾ cup.

Chocolate Glaze

¼ cup butter or margarine	2 cups sifted powdered sugar
2 (1-ounce) squares unsweetened chocolate	3 tablespoons hot water
	1 teaspoon vanilla extract

Combine butter and chocolate in a heavy saucepan. Cook over low heat until chocolate melts, stirring occasionally. Remove from heat. Add powdered sugar, hot water, and vanilla, beating at high speed of an electric mixer until smooth. **Yield:** 1 cup.

DIXIE GENERAL'S CAKE

HOT CHOCOLATE SOUFFLÉ

Cakes, Pies & Other Desserts

CHOCOLATE MOUSSE CAKE

Marbled Dessert Loaf

Sifting cocoa

- Sift cocoa over half of cake batter. A tea strainer like this helps prevent a mess on your countertop.

Swirling batters

- Swirl first 2 layers of batter together with a kitchen knife; then top with remaining batters, and swirl again.

¾ cup butter or margarine, softened
2 (3-ounce) packages cream cheese, softened
1⅓ cups sugar
4 large eggs
1½ cups all-purpose flour
1 teaspoon baking powder
½ teaspoon salt
1 tablespoon vanilla extract
¼ cup cocoa

Beat butter and cream cheese at medium speed of an electric mixer until creamy; gradually add sugar, beating until light and fluffy. Add eggs, one at a time, beating well after each addition.

Combine flour, baking powder, and salt; add to creamed mixture, beating until well blended. Stir in vanilla. Pour half of batter into a separate bowl. Sift cocoa over half of batter; beat at low speed until blended. Spoon half of chocolate batter into a greased 9- x 5- x 3-inch loafpan; top with half of vanilla batter. Swirl batters together with a knife to create a marbled effect. Top with remaining chocolate batter and vanilla batter. Swirl batters again.

Bake at 350° for 45 minutes. Cover with aluminum foil, and bake 20 additional minutes or until a wooden pick inserted in center comes out clean. Let cool in pan 10 minutes. Remove from pan, and let cool completely on a wire rack. **Yield:** one 9-inch loaf.

Whipping Cream Pound Cake

1 cup butter or margarine,
  softened
3 cups sugar
6 large eggs
3 cups sifted cake flour

1 cup whipping cream
2 teaspoons vanilla extract
Powdered sugar
Garnishes: fresh strawberries,
  fresh mint sprigs

Beat butter at medium speed of an electric mixer until creamy; gradually add 3 cups sugar, beating well. Add eggs, one at a time, beating after each addition. Add flour to creamed mixture alternately with whipping cream, beginning and ending with flour. Mix just until blended after each addition. Stir in vanilla.

  Pour batter into a greased and floured 10-inch Bundt pan. Bake at 325° for 1 hour and 15 minutes. Let cool in pan 10 minutes. Remove from pan; let cool completely on a wire rack. Sift powdered sugar over cake. Garnish, if desired. **Yield:** one 10-inch cake.

EQUIPMENT NEEDED:
• Electric mixer
• 10-inch Bundt pan
• Sifter
• Wire cooling rack

Extract options
• You can change the flavor of this classic cake by omitting the vanilla and substituting another flavoring such as lemon, orange, or rum.

About flour
• Cake flour is a delicate soft wheat flour. For the most accurate measurement, always sift cake flour before measuring it. If you choose to substitute all-purpose flour, use 2 tablespoons less per cup. All-purpose flour is presifted, so don't sift it again.

EQUIPMENT NEEDED:

- 10-inch cast-iron skillet
- Electric mixer

Brown sugar glaze

- Sprinkle brown sugar over melted butter in skillet. The mixture will form a glaze as the cake bakes.

Placing pineapple

- Arrange pineapple pieces snugly in a spoke fashion around whole slice of pineapple, and cut side up around sides of skillet.

Pineapple Upside-Down Cake

½ cup butter or margarine	1 cup sugar
1 cup firmly packed brown sugar	1 cup all-purpose flour
3 (8¼-ounce) cans pineapple slices, undrained	1 teaspoon baking powder
10 pecan halves	½ teaspoon ground cinnamon
11 maraschino cherries, halved	¼ teaspoon salt
2 large eggs, separated	1 teaspoon vanilla extract
1 egg yolk	¼ teaspoon cream of tartar

Melt butter in a 10-inch cast-iron skillet over low heat. Sprinkle brown sugar in skillet. Remove from heat.

Drain pineapple, reserving ¼ cup juice. Set juice aside. Cut pineapple slices in half, reserving 1 whole slice. Place whole pineapple slice in center of skillet. Arrange 10 pineapple pieces spoke fashion around whole slice in center of skillet. Place a pecan half and a cherry half between each piece of pineapple. Place a cherry half in center of whole pineapple slice. Arrange remaining pineapple pieces, cut side up, around sides of skillet. Place a cherry half in center of each piece of pineapple around sides of skillet.

Beat 3 egg yolks at high speed of an electric mixer until thick and lemon colored; gradually add 1 cup sugar, beating well. Combine flour and next 3 ingredients; stir well. Add to egg mixture alternately with reserved ¼ cup pineapple juice. Stir in vanilla.

Beat egg whites and cream of tartar at high speed of mixer until stiff peaks form; fold beaten egg whites into batter. Spoon batter evenly over pineapple in skillet. Bake at 350° for 45 to 50 minutes or until cake is set. Invert cake onto a serving plate. Scrape any remaining glaze from skillet onto cake. Cut into wedges to serve. **Yield:** one 10-inch cake.

Strawberry Shortcakes

2 cups sliced fresh strawberries
3 tablespoons sugar
½ teaspoon ground cinnamon
3 cups biscuit and baking mix
3 tablespoons sugar
½ cup plus 2 tablespoons milk
3 tablespoons butter or
    margarine, melted

1 teaspoon sugar
½ cup strawberry preserves
2 tablespoons strawberry
    schnapps, divided
½ cup whipping cream
¼ cup sifted powdered sugar
Garnishes: fresh blueberries,
    fresh mint sprigs

EQUIPMENT NEEDED:
- Rolling pin
- 4-inch round cutter
- Baking sheet
- Electric mixer or wire whisk
- Sifter

Place strawberries in a large bowl. Combine 3 tablespoons sugar and cinnamon; stir well. Sprinkle cinnamon-sugar mixture over strawberries; toss gently. Set aside. Combine biscuit mix and 3 tablespoons sugar in a large bowl. Add milk and butter, stirring with a fork until mixture forms a soft dough. Turn dough out onto a lightly floured surface; knead 4 or 5 times. Roll dough to ½-inch thickness; cut into four 4-inch circles, using a cookie cutter. Place circles on an ungreased baking sheet; sprinkle with 1 teaspoon sugar.

    Bake at 425° for 10 to 12 minutes or until golden. Gently split warm shortcakes horizontally with a fork.

    Combine strawberry preserves and 1 tablespoon schnapps in a small bowl; stir well. Spread 2 tablespoons preserves mixture on each cut side of bottom halves of shortcakes. Spoon ½ cup strawberry mixture over preserves mixture on each bottom half. Top each with top half of shortcake, cut side down.

    Beat whipping cream until foamy; gradually add powdered sugar, beating until soft peaks form. Fold in remaining 1 tablespoon schnapps. Top each shortcake with a dollop of whipped cream. Garnish, if desired. **Yield:** 4 servings.

Biscuit cutters

- Round metal biscuit cutters are available in graduated sets in many kitchen shops or grocery stores.

Sweetening berries

- Sprinkle cinnamon-sugar mixture over sliced berries. Upon standing, the mixture will form a syrup.

Splitting shortcakes

- Gently split warm shortcakes in half. A fork works best for this easy task.

Alabama Lane Cake

1 cup butter, softened
2 cups sugar
3¼ cups sifted cake flour
1 tablespoon baking powder
¾ teaspoon salt
½ cup milk

½ cup half-and-half
1½ teaspoons vanilla extract
8 egg whites
Cherry Filling
Fluffy Frosting

EQUIPMENT NEEDED:
• Electric mixer
• Three 9-inch cakepans
• Wire cooling racks
• Heavy saucepan
• Double boiler

Beat butter at medium speed of an electric mixer until creamy; gradually add sugar, beating well. Combine flour, baking powder, and salt; add to creamed mixture alternately with milk and half-and-half, beginning and ending with flour mixture. Beat well after each addition. Stir in vanilla.

Beat egg whites at high speed of mixer until stiff peaks form; gently fold into batter. Pour batter into three greased and floured 9-inch round cakepans.

Bake at 375° for 20 minutes or until a wooden pick inserted in center comes out clean. Let cool in pans 10 minutes; remove from pans, and let cool completely on wire racks. Spread Cherry Filling between layers and on top of cake. Spread Fluffy Frosting on sides of cake. **Yield:** one 3-layer cake.

Save your yolks
• Don't discard the 8 yolks once you've separated the eggs; you'll use them in the Cherry Filling.

Get the red out

• Press cherries between paper towels to remove excess moisture and to keep them from staining the white frosting.

Cherry Filling

½ cup sliced or halved
   maraschino cherries
1¼ cups sugar
½ cup butter
8 egg yolks, lightly beaten

1 cup chopped pecans
1 cup raisins
1 cup flaked coconut
¼ cup bourbon

Press cherries between paper towels to remove excess moisture; set aside. Combine sugar, butter, and egg yolks in a heavy saucepan. Cook over medium heat, stirring constantly, 20 minutes or until butter melts and mixture is very thick. Stir in cherries, pecans, and remaining ingredients. Let cool completely. **Yield:** 3⅓ cups.

Seven-minute frosting

• Place frosting over boiling water; beat constantly at high speed 7 minutes.

Fluffy Frosting

¾ cup sugar
2 tablespoons plus 2 teaspoons
   water
1 egg white

1½ teaspoons light corn syrup
Dash of salt
½ teaspoon vanilla extract

Combine first 5 ingredients in top of a double boiler; beat at low speed of an electric mixer just until blended. Place frosting over boiling water; beat constantly at high speed 7 minutes or until stiff peaks form. Remove from heat. Add vanilla; beat 1 additional minute or until spreading consistency. Spread immediately. **Yield:** 2 cups.

Black Forest Cake

EQUIPMENT NEEDED:
- Sifter
- Two 9-inch cakepans
- Electric mixer
- Wire cooling racks
- Food processor

Cake crumbs

• Split cake layers in half horizontally, and make fine crumbs from 1 layer by pulsing cake pieces in food processor for a few seconds.

• Carefully press fine cake crumbs generously onto sides of frosted cake.

2 cups sifted cake flour
1¼ teaspoons baking powder
¼ teaspoon baking soda
¾ teaspoon salt
2 cups sugar
¾ cup cocoa
½ cup shortening
½ cup sour cream, divided
½ cup milk
⅓ cup kirsch or other
    cherry-flavored brandy

2 large eggs
2 egg yolks
4 cups whipping cream
⅓ cup sifted powdered sugar
2 tablespoons kirsch or other
    cherry-flavored brandy
2 (21-ounce) cans cherry pie
    filling

Grease two 9-inch round cakepans; line bottoms with wax paper. Grease and flour wax paper and sides of pans. Set aside.

Combine first 6 ingredients in a large mixing bowl; stir well. Add shortening and ¼ cup sour cream. Beat at low speed of an electric mixer 30 seconds or until dry ingredients are moistened. Add remaining ¼ cup sour cream, milk, and ⅓ cup kirsch. Beat at medium speed 1½ minutes. Add eggs and egg yolks, one at a time, beating 20 seconds after each addition. Pour batter into prepared pans.

Bake at 350° for 30 to 35 minutes or until a wooden pick inserted in center comes out clean. Let cool in pans 10 minutes; remove from pans. Peel off wax paper, and let cake layers cool on wire racks.

Split cake layers in half horizontally to make 4 layers. Position knife blade in food processor bowl. Break 1 cake layer into pieces, and place in processor bowl. Pulse 5 or 6 times or until cake resembles fine crumbs. Set crumbs aside.

Beat whipping cream until foamy; gradually add powdered sugar, beating until soft peaks form. Add 2 tablespoons kirsch, beating until stiff peaks form. Reserve 1½ cups whipped cream mixture for garnish.

Place 1 cake layer on a cake plate, cut side up; spread with 1 cup whipped cream mixture, and top with 1 cup pie filling. Repeat procedure once, and top with remaining cake layer. Frost sides and top of cake with whipped cream mixture. Carefully pat cake crumbs generously around sides of frosted cake. Pipe or spoon reserved 1½ cups whipped cream mixture around top edges of cake; spoon 1 cup pie filling in center. (Reserve any remaining pie filling for another use.) Cover and chill cake 8 hours before serving. **Yield:** one 3-layer cake.

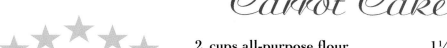

Carrot Cake Supreme

⭐⭐⭐⭐⭐

EQUIPMENT NEEDED:
- Three 9-inch cakepans
- Electric mixer
- Wire cooling racks
- Food processor or grater

Shredding carrots
- The shredder disc of a food processor makes thin shreds of carrot. You can use a small hand grater, if desired.

- Combine coconut and ½ cup shredded carrot, and gently press onto sides and on top of frosted cake.

2 cups all-purpose flour
1½ teaspoons baking soda
1 teaspoon baking powder
¼ teaspoon salt
2 cups sugar
1¼ teaspoons ground cinnamon
¾ teaspoon ground ginger
¾ teaspoon ground nutmeg

1¼ cups vegetable oil
4 large eggs
2½ cups finely shredded carrot, divided
½ cup chopped pecans
1 teaspoon vanilla extract
Cream Cheese Frosting
1 (3½-ounce) can flaked coconut

Grease and flour three 9-inch round cakepans. Line with wax paper; grease paper, and set aside.

Combine first 8 ingredients; stir. Add oil and eggs, beating well at medium speed of an electric mixer. Stir in 2 cups shredded carrot, pecans, and vanilla. Spoon batter into prepared cakepans.

Bake at 350° for 30 to 35 minutes or until a wooden pick inserted near center comes out clean. Let cool in pans 10 minutes; remove layers from pans. Peel off wax paper; let cool completely on wire racks. Spread Cream Cheese Frosting between layers and on top and sides of cake. Combine coconut and remaining ½ cup shredded carrot. Gently press onto sides of cake, and sprinkle over top. **Yield:** one 3-layer cake.

Cream Cheese Frosting

1 (8-ounce) package cream cheese, softened
½ cup butter or margarine, softened

1 (16-ounce) package powdered sugar, sifted
2 teaspoons vanilla extract
1 to 2 teaspoons milk

Beat cream cheese and butter at medium speed of an electric mixer until smooth. Gradually add powdered sugar, beating until well blended. Stir in vanilla. Add milk, 1 teaspoon at a time, stirring until frosting is spreading consistency. **Yield:** 2¾ cups.

Dixie General's Cake

2 cups sifted cake flour
1½ teaspoons baking powder
⅛ teaspoon salt
9 large eggs, separated
2 cups sugar
½ cup vegetable oil

2 teaspoons grated lemon rind
2 tablespoons lemon juice
½ teaspoon cream of tartar
Orange-Lemon Frosting
Garnishes: lemon slices, orange
    slices, fresh mint sprigs

Grease and flour four 8-inch round cakepans. Line with wax paper; grease paper, and set aside.

Combine first 3 ingredients; stir well. Combine egg yolks and sugar in a large mixing bowl; beat at high speed of an electric mixer until thick and lemon colored. Gradually add oil, beating at medium speed. Add flour mixture, mixing until blended. Stir in lemon rind and juice. Set aside.

Beat egg whites and cream of tartar at high speed until stiff peaks form. Gently stir one-fourth of egg white mixture into batter. Gently fold in remaining egg white mixture. Pour batter into prepared pans.

Bake at 325° for 20 to 25 minutes or until a wooden pick inserted in center comes out clean. Let cool in pans 10 minutes. Remove from pans; peel off wax paper, and let cool completely on wire racks.

Spread Orange-Lemon Frosting between layers and on top and sides of cake. Chill thoroughly. Garnish, if desired. **Yield:** one 4-layer cake.

Orange-Lemon Frosting

½ cup butter or margarine,
    softened
2 tablespoons sour cream
2 (16-ounce) packages powdered
    sugar, sifted
¼ cup grated orange rind
    (4 oranges)

1 tablespoon plus 1 teaspoon
    grated lemon rind (2 lemons)
3 to 4 tablespoons orange juice
2 tablespoons lemon juice

Beat butter at medium speed of an electric mixer until creamy; stir in sour cream. Add powdered sugar and grated rinds alternately with juices, beating until mixture is smooth. **Yield:** 4 cups.

Italian Cream Cake

1 cup butter or margarine, softened
2 cups sugar
5 large eggs, separated
2½ cups all-purpose flour
1 teaspoon baking soda
1 cup buttermilk
⅔ cup finely chopped pecans
1 teaspoon vanilla extract
1 (3½-ounce) can flaked coconut
½ teaspoon cream of tartar
3 tablespoons light rum
Cream Cheese Frosting

Grease and flour three 9-inch round cakepans. Line pans with wax paper; grease paper, and set aside.

Beat butter at medium speed of an electric mixer until creamy; gradually add sugar, beating well. Add egg yolks, one at a time, beating after each addition. Combine flour and baking soda. Add to creamed mixture alternately with buttermilk, beginning and ending with flour mixture. Stir in pecans, vanilla, and coconut.

Beat egg whites at high speed in a large bowl until foamy. Add cream of tartar; beat until stiff peaks form. Gently fold beaten egg whites into batter. Pour batter into prepared pans.

Bake at 350° for 25 to 30 minutes or until a wooden pick inserted in center comes out clean. Let cool in pans 10 minutes. Remove from pans; peel off wax paper, and let cool completely on wire racks. Sprinkle each cake layer with 1 tablespoon light rum. Let stand 10 minutes. Spread Cream Cheese Frosting between layers and on sides and top of cake. **Yield:** one 3-layer cake.

Cream Cheese Frosting

1 (8-ounce) package cream cheese, softened
1 (3-ounce) package cream cheese, softened
¾ cup butter, softened
1½ (16-ounce) packages powdered sugar, sifted
1½ cups chopped pecans
1 tablespoon vanilla extract

Beat first 3 ingredients at medium speed of electric mixer until smooth. Gradually add powdered sugar, beating until light and fluffy. Stir in pecans and vanilla. **Yield:** enough for one 3-layer cake.

EQUIPMENT NEEDED:
- Three 9-inch cakepans
- Electric mixer
- Wire cooling racks
- Large spatula

Adding rum

- Sprinkle each cake layer with rum to add extra moistness and flavor.

Spreading frosting

- Spread frosting on top of cake last so that the cake will stand evenly.

EQUIPMENT NEEDED:

- Sifter
- Electric mixer
- 10-inch tube pan
- Rubber spatula
- Long metal spatula or table knife

Folding in flour

- Sprinkle flour over beaten egg whites a little at a time, and gently fold in. This keeps egg whites from deflating.

Swirling batter

- Drop batters alternately by large spoonfuls into ungreased tube pan; gently swirl with a knife.

Daffodil Sponge Cake

1 cup sifted cake flour	½ teaspoon salt
½ cup sugar	¾ cup sugar
4 egg yolks	½ teaspoon vanilla extract
½ teaspoon lemon extract	Lemon Glaze
10 egg whites	Garnishes: lemon roses, fresh
1 teaspoon cream of tartar	lemon balm leaves

Sift flour and ½ cup sugar together three times; set aside. Beat egg yolks at high speed of an electric mixer 4 minutes or until thick and lemon colored. Add lemon extract; beat at medium speed 5 minutes or until thick.

Beat egg whites, cream of tartar, and salt at high speed of mixer just until foamy. Gradually add ¾ cup sugar, 2 tablespoons at a time, beating mixture until stiff peaks form and sugar dissolves (2 to 4 minutes).

Sprinkle one-fourth of flour mixture over beaten egg whites; gently fold in, using a rubber spatula. Repeat procedure with remaining flour mixture, adding one-fourth of mixture at a time. Divide egg white mixture in half. Gently fold vanilla into half of egg white mixture. Gently fold beaten egg yolk mixture into remaining half of egg white mixture. Drop batters alternately by spoonfuls into an ungreased 10-inch tube pan. Swirl batters with a knife to create a marbled effect.

Bake at 350° for 45 to 50 minutes or until cake springs back when touched. Invert pan. Let cake cool in pan 40 minutes. Loosen cake from sides of pan, using a narrow metal spatula; remove cake from pan. Place cake on a serving plate. Drizzle with Lemon Glaze. Garnish, if desired. **Yield:** one 10-inch cake.

Lemon Glaze

1½ cups sifted powdered sugar	⅛ teaspoon lemon extract
1 teaspoon grated lemon rind	2 to 3 tablespoons lemon juice

Combine all ingredients, stirring until smooth. **Yield:** about ½ cup.

Classic Cherry Cheesecake

1½ cups graham cracker crumbs
2 tablespoons sugar
¼ cup plus 2 tablespoons butter
    or margarine, melted
1 teaspoon grated lemon rind
3 (8-ounce) packages cream
    cheese, softened
1 cup sugar

3 large eggs
½ teaspoon vanilla extract
1 (16-ounce) carton sour cream
3 tablespoons sugar
½ teaspoon vanilla extract
1 (21-ounce) can cherry pie
    filling

EQUIPMENT NEEDED:
• Rolling pin (optional)
• 9-inch springform pan
• Electric mixer
• Wire cooling rack
• Rubber spatula

Combine first 4 ingredients in a medium bowl; stir well. Press mixture firmly on bottom and up sides of a 9-inch springform pan. Bake at 350° for 5 minutes; set aside.

Beat cream cheese at high speed of an electric mixer until light and fluffy; gradually add 1 cup sugar, beating well. Add eggs, one at a time, beating well after each addition; stir in ½ teaspoon vanilla. Pour cream cheese mixture into prepared crust. Bake at 375° for 30 to 35 minutes or until cheesecake is set.

Beat sour cream at medium speed 2 minutes. Add 3 tablespoons sugar and ½ teaspoon vanilla; beat 1 additional minute. Spread sour cream mixture evenly over cheesecake. Bake at 500° for 3 to 5 minutes or until sour cream mixture is bubbly. Remove cheesecake from oven. Let cool to room temperature in pan on a wire rack. Top with pie filling. Cover and chill at least 8 hours. To serve, carefully remove sides of springform pan. **Yield:** 10 to 12 servings.

Making crumbs

• Use commercial graham cracker crumbs for crumb crust, or crush whole graham crackers in a zip-top plastic bag, using a rolling pin.

Sour cream top

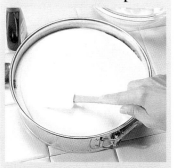

• Spread sour cream mixture evenly over baked cheesecake, and bake at 500° for 3 to 5 minutes longer to set the topping.

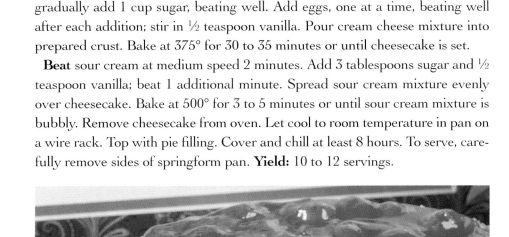

Chocolate Mousse Cake

Doily design

- Place a paper doily over whipped cream frosted cake, and sift cocoa over doily.

- Carefully lift doily off cake to reveal design. Discard doily.

8 (1-ounce) squares semisweet chocolate
1 (8-ounce) package cream cheese, softened
1 (3-ounce) package cream cheese, softened
⅔ cup sugar
6 large eggs
⅓ cup whipping cream
1 tablespoon vanilla extract
Chocolate Crust
Whipped Cream Topping
2 teaspoons cocoa

Place chocolate in top of a double boiler; bring water to a boil. Reduce heat to low; cook until chocolate melts. Remove from heat, and let cool.

Combine cream cheese and sugar in a large mixing bowl, and beat at medium speed of an electric mixer until light and fluffy. Add eggs, one at a time, beating after each addition. Add melted chocolate, whipping cream, and vanilla; beat at low speed just until blended. Pour into Chocolate Crust. Bake at 375° for 30 to 35 minutes or just until outside edges are firm but center is still soft. Let cool to room temperature; cover and chill at least 8 hours.

Spread cake with Whipped Cream Topping. Remove cake from pan. Place a paper doily on top; sift cocoa over it. Carefully lift doily off cake. **Yield:** one 9-inch cake.

Chocolate Crust

½ cup butter or margarine
3 (1-ounce) squares semisweet chocolate
1½ cups fine, dry breadcrumbs
⅓ cup sugar

Combine butter and chocolate in top of a double boiler; bring water to a boil. Reduce heat to low; cook until chocolate melts. Remove from heat.

Add breadcrumbs and sugar to chocolate mixture, blending well. Press into bottom and 2 inches up sides of a greased 9-inch springform pan. Bake at 350° for 5 minutes. Let cool. Refrigerate until chilled. **Yield:** one 9-inch crust.

Whipped Cream Topping

1½ cups whipping cream
¼ cup sifted powdered sugar
½ teaspoon vanilla extract

Beat whipping cream at high speed of an electric mixer until foamy; gradually add powdered sugar, beating until soft peaks form. Add vanilla; beat well. Cover and chill. **Yield:** 3 cups.

Rich White Chocolate Cheesecake

2 cups chocolate wafer crumbs	4 large eggs
2 tablespoons sugar	½ cup Irish Cream liqueur or
⅓ cup butter or margarine, melted	half-and-half
	1 tablespoon vanilla extract
4 (8-ounce) packages cream cheese, softened	½ pound premium white chocolate, chopped
1 cup sugar	Garnish: marbled chocolate curls

Combine first 3 ingredients in a medium bowl; stir well. Press mixture firmly on bottom and 2 inches up sides of a 10-inch springform pan. Bake at 325° for 6 to 8 minutes. Set aside to cool.

Beat cream cheese at medium speed of an electric mixer until smooth. Add 1 cup sugar, beating well. Add eggs, one at a time, beating just until blended after each addition. Stir in liqueur and vanilla. Add white chocolate; stir well. Pour mixture into prepared crust. Bake at 325° for 50 to 60 minutes or until set. Turn oven off. Partially open oven door. Leave cheesecake in oven 1 hour. Remove cheesecake from oven; let cool to room temperature in pan on a wire rack. Cover and chill thoroughly. To serve, remove sides of springform pan. Garnish, if desired. (See note below and photos.) **Yield:** one 10-inch cheesecake.

Note: To make marbled chocolate curls, melt 12 ounces semisweet chocolate in top of a double boiler over hot water. Pour onto a smooth surface like marble or an aluminum foil-lined baking sheet. Melt 12 ounces white chocolate, and pour over semisweet chocolate layer. Using a small spatula, swirl chocolates to create a marbled effect, covering about a 12- x 9-inch area. Let swirled chocolate stand at room temperature until it feels slightly tacky but not firm. (If chocolate is too hard, curls will break; if too soft, chocolate will not curl.) Pull a cheese plane across chocolate to form curls.

EQUIPMENT NEEDED:

- 10-inch springform pan
- Electric mixer
- Wire cooling rack
- Double boiler (optional)
- Marble slab or baking sheet (optional)
- Cheese plane or vegetable peeler (optional)

Making marbled curls

- To make chocolate curls, swirl chocolates to create a marbled effect, using a small metal spatula.

- Let swirled chocolate stand until slightly tacky but not hard. Pull a cheese plane or large vegetable peeler across chocolate to form large curls.

Mocha-Pecan Torte

EQUIPMENT NEEDED:
- Four 8-inch cakepans
- Electric mixer
- Wire cooling racks
- Decorating bag or parchment paper and No. 2F metal tip

Piping frosting

- Spoon frosting into a decorating bag fitted with a large metal tip. Pipe rosettes around top edge of torte. Or make your own bag. Roll a square of parchment paper into a cone, and snip a hole in the end; insert metal tip.

8 large eggs, separated
⅔ cup sifted powdered sugar
1 teaspoon baking powder
⅓ cup cocoa
⅓ cup soft breadcrumbs
1 teaspoon vanilla extract
2 cups ground pecans
Mocha Buttercream Frosting
Chocolate candy sprinkles

Line bottoms of four 8-inch round cakepans with wax paper. Grease and flour wax paper; set pans aside.

Combine egg yolks, sugar, and baking powder in a large bowl; beat at high speed of an electric mixer 2 to 3 minutes or until mixture is thick and lemon colored. Combine cocoa and breadcrumbs, and stir into egg yolk mixture. Stir in vanilla; fold in pecans.

Beat egg whites in a mixing bowl until stiff peaks form; gently fold one-fourth of egg whites into yolk mixture. Fold remaining egg whites into yolk mixture. Pour batter evenly into prepared pans; smooth top of batter.

Bake at 350° for 15 minutes or until layers spring back when lightly touched. (Do not overbake.) Let cool in pans 5 minutes. Invert layers onto wire racks, and gently peel off wax paper. (Layers will be thin.) Let cool completely.

Set aside 1½ cups Mocha Buttercream Frosting for piping. Spread remaining 3 cups frosting between layers and on top and sides of torte. Gently pat chocolate sprinkles onto sides of torte. Lightly score frosting on top of torte into 12 wedges.

Spoon reserved 1½ cups frosting into a large decorating bag fitted with a No. 2F metal tip. Pipe 12 rosettes of frosting evenly around top edge of torte (or dollop frosting around edge); sprinkle rosettes with chocolate sprinkles. Chill thoroughly. **Yield:** one 8-inch torte.

Mocha Buttercream Frosting

2½ teaspoons instant coffee granules
2 tablespoons hot water
¾ cup plus 2 tablespoons butter, softened
1 tablespoon plus 2 teaspoons cocoa
7 cups sifted powdered sugar
⅓ cup half-and-half
1 teaspoon vanilla extract

Dissolve coffee granules in water; let cool. Beat butter in a large bowl at high speed until creamy. Add coffee and cocoa; beat until blended. Gradually add sugar alternately with half-and-half, beating until light and fluffy. Stir in vanilla. **Yield:** 4½ cups.

Toffee Meringue Torte

6 egg whites
¾ teaspoon cream of tartar
1 cup superfine sugar
8 (1.4-ounce) English
    toffee-flavored candy bars,
    frozen and crushed

2½ cups whipping cream,
    whipped
Toffee Sauce

Line two baking sheets with parchment paper. Trace a 9-inch circle on each piece of paper, using a 9-inch round cakepan as a guide. Turn paper over, and set aside.

Beat egg whites at high speed of an electric mixer until foamy; add cream of tartar, beating until soft peaks form. Gradually add sugar, 2 tablespoons at a time, beating until stiff peaks form (2 to 4 minutes). Spoon meringue mixture evenly inside circles on prepared baking sheets. Form mixture on each sheet into a smooth circle, spreading with the back of a large spoon. Bake at 275° for 2 hours. Turn oven off, and let cool slightly. Remove from oven, and peel off paper. Let meringues dry completely on wire racks, away from drafts.

Reserve 2 tablespoons crushed candy for garnish. Gradually fold remaining crushed candy into whipped cream. Chill or freeze until firm but spreadable. Spread whipped cream mixture between layers and on top and sides of meringue. Garnish with reserved crushed candy. Place torte in an airtight cake cover, and freeze at least 8 hours. Cut into wedges, and serve with warm Toffee Sauce. **Yield:** 8 to 10 servings.

Toffee Sauce

1½ cups firmly packed brown
    sugar
½ cup light corn syrup

⅓ cup butter
⅔ cup whipping cream
1 teaspoon butter flavoring

Combine first 3 ingredients in a saucepan. Cook over medium heat until mixture comes to a full boil (about 5 minutes), stirring often. Remove from heat, and let cool 5 minutes. Stir in whipping cream and butter flavoring. Serve warm with torte. **Yield:** 2 cups.

EQUIPMENT NEEDED:
- Two baking sheets
- Parchment paper
- 9-inch round cakepan or 9-inch plate
- Electric mixer
- Wire cooling racks
- Saucepan

Freeze and crush
- Frozen toffee-flavored candy bars are easy to crush. Just leave them in their wrappers, and tap them on the counter-top several times.

Shaping meringue circles

- Spoon meringue mixture evenly inside the circles drawn on parchment paper.

Apple Cobbler à la Mode

6 cups peeled, sliced cooking apples

1½ cups chopped walnuts, divided

½ cup firmly packed brown sugar

1 teaspoon ground cinnamon

1 cup all-purpose flour

1 teaspoon baking powder

¼ teaspoon salt

1 cup sugar

¼ teaspoon ground ginger

1 large egg, lightly beaten

½ cup half-and-half

½ cup butter or margarine, melted

Vanilla ice cream

Place apple, 1 cup walnuts, brown sugar, and cinnamon in a large bowl; toss gently. Spread apple mixture in a greased 11- x 7- x 1½-inch baking dish. Set aside.

Combine flour and next 4 ingredients in a large bowl; stir well. Combine egg, half-and-half, and melted butter; stir well. Add egg mixture to dry ingredients, stirring just until blended. Pour batter over apple mixture; sprinkle with remaining ½ cup chopped walnuts.

Bake at 350° for 45 minutes to 1 hour or until lightly browned. To serve, spoon warm cobbler into individual serving bowls. Top each serving with vanilla ice cream. **Yield:** 8 servings.

Pouring batter

• Pour batter over apple mixture in dish.

Cooking apples

• Common cooking apples include Granny Smith (shown), Rome Beauty, Golden Delicious, McIntosh, or Jonathan. One medium apple should yield 1 cup slices.

Apple Dumplings

EQUIPMENT NEEDED:
- Pastry blender or two knives
- Rolling pin
- Fluted pastry wheel
- Apple corer or small knife
- 13- x 9- x 2-inch baking dish

Coring apples

- Peel and core apples, and cut each in half crosswise. (If you don't have an apple corer, peel and cut apples in half, and then trim out the core with a knife.)

Wrapping apples

- Moisten edges of each pastry square with water; then bring corners to the center over the apple half, and press edges to seal.

3 cups all-purpose flour	1 tablespoon sugar
2 teaspoons baking powder	1½ teaspoons ground cinnamon
1 teaspoon salt	1½ cups sugar
1 cup shortening	1 cup orange juice
¾ cup milk	½ cup water
3 large Granny Smith, Winesap, or other cooking apples	1 tablespoon butter or margarine
2 tablespoons butter or margarine	¼ teaspoon ground cinnamon
	¼ teaspoon ground nutmeg

Combine first 3 ingredients; cut in shortening with a pastry blender until mixture is crumbly. Gradually add milk, stirring with a fork until dry ingredients are moistened. Shape into a ball. Roll pastry to ¼-inch thickness on a lightly floured surface, shaping into a 21- x 14-inch rectangle. Cut pastry into six 7-inch squares with a fluted pastry wheel.

Peel and core apples; cut each in half crosswise. Place 1 apple half, cut side down, on each pastry square; dot each apple half with 1 teaspoon butter. Sprinkle each with ½ teaspoon sugar and ¼ teaspoon cinnamon. Moisten edges of each pastry square with water; bring corners to center, pressing edges to seal. Place dumplings in a lightly greased 13- x 9- x 2-inch baking dish. Bake at 375° for 35 minutes or until apples are tender and pastry is lightly browned.

Combine 1½ cups sugar and remaining 5 ingredients in a medium saucepan. Bring to a boil; reduce heat, and simmer, uncovered, 4 minutes or until butter melts and sugar dissolves, stirring occasionally. Pour syrup over dumplings, and serve immediately. **Yield:** 6 servings.

EQUIPMENT NEEDED:

- 2½-quart shallow baking dish
- Pastry blender or two knives
- Electric mixer

Preparing peaches

- Sprinkle lemon juice over sliced peaches to prevent browning.

Cutting up butter

- Cut butter into oat mixture with a pastry blender until butter is well distributed and mixture is crumbly.

Peach Crumble

10 to 12 cups peeled, sliced fresh ripe peaches
2 tablespoons lemon juice
1 cup firmly packed brown sugar
¾ cup regular oats, uncooked
3 tablespoons all-purpose flour
¾ teaspoon ground cinnamon
⅛ teaspoon ground nutmeg
Dash of salt
Dash of allspice
⅔ cup butter or margarine
Spiced Cream
¼ cup chopped blanched almonds, toasted

Place peach slices in a lightly greased 2½-quart shallow baking dish. Sprinkle with lemon juice; toss gently to coat evenly.

Combine sugar and next 6 ingredients in a medium bowl; stir well. Cut in butter with a pastry blender until mixture is crumbly. Sprinkle topping evenly over peaches. Bake at 350° for 25 to 30 minutes or until peaches are tender and topping is lightly browned. Serve warm with Spiced Cream. Sprinkle each serving with almonds. **Yield:** 8 to 10 servings.

Spiced Cream

¾ cup whipping cream
2 tablespoons powdered sugar
½ teaspoon ground cinnamon
¼ teaspoon vanilla extract

Beat whipping cream at high speed of an electric mixer until foamy; add sugar, cinnamon, and vanilla, beating until stiff peaks form. **Yield:** 1⅔ cups.

Transferring pastry

• To transfer pastry to pieplate, gently roll pastry onto a rolling pin; then carefully unroll pastry into pieplate. This prevents pastry from tearing.

Coating berries

• Coat blueberries with cornstarch, and sprinkle berries over filling. This light coating prevents berries from discoloring the filling.

Streusel-Topped Blueberry Cream Pie

2 cups all-purpose flour	2 tablespoons lemon juice
3 tablespoons sugar	½ teaspoon salt
½ teaspoon salt	1 (16-ounce) carton sour cream
¾ cup butter, chilled	3 cups fresh or frozen blueberries, thawed
2 egg yolks	
5 to 6 tablespoons water	2 tablespoons cornstarch
2 large eggs	½ cup all-purpose flour
2 (3-ounce) packages cream cheese, softened	½ cup firmly packed brown sugar
¾ cup sugar	½ teaspoon ground cinnamon
¼ cup plus 1 tablespoon all-purpose flour	¼ cup butter or margarine, chilled
1 teaspoon grated lemon rind	½ cup coarsely chopped walnuts

Combine first 3 ingredients; stir well. Cut in ¾ cup butter with a pastry blender just until mixture is crumbly. Stir in 2 egg yolks and water, 1 tablespoon at a time, until dough forms a ball. Cover and chill at least 30 minutes. Roll pastry to about ⅛-inch thickness on a floured surface. Place in a 9-inch deep-dish pieplate. Fold edges under, and flute.

Combine 2 eggs and cream cheese; beat at medium speed of an electric mixer until smooth. Add ¾ cup sugar and next 5 ingredients. Stir well. Pour mixture into prepared pastry. Coat blueberries with cornstarch. Sprinkle coated blueberries over filling. Bake at 400° for 10 minutes.

Combine ½ cup flour, brown sugar, and cinnamon. Cut in ¼ cup butter until mixture is crumbly. Add walnuts. Sprinkle over partially baked pie. Bake 25 additional minutes, shielding crust with aluminum foil to prevent excessive browning, if necessary. Let cool before slicing. **Yield:** one 9-inch deep-dish pie.

Easy Lemon Chess Pie

1¾ cups sugar
2 tablespoons yellow cornmeal
¼ teaspoon salt
⅓ cup butter or margarine, melted

¼ cup evaporated milk
3 tablespoons lemon juice
4 large eggs
½ (15-ounce) package refrigerated piecrusts

Combine first 3 ingredients in a medium bowl, stirring well. Add butter, milk, and lemon juice; stir well. Add eggs, one at a time, beating well after each addition.

Fit piecrust into a 9-inch pieplate according to package directions; flute edges. Pour filling mixture into piecrust. Bake at 350° for 45 to 50 minutes or until pie is set. Let cool on a wire rack. **Yield:** one 9-inch pie.

EQUIPMENT NEEDED:
• 9-inch pieplate
• Wire cooling rack

Fluting with a fork

• Fit commercial pastry into pieplate according to package directions. Use a fork to flute a homemade-looking crust.

Harvest Pumpkin Pie

EQUIPMENT NEEDED:

- Rolling pin
- 10-inch pieplate
- Wire whisk
- Baking sheet
- Wire cooling rack
- Electric mixer

Making leaves

• Cut leaf shapes from half of pastry; make vein markings on leaves, using the back of a small knife.

Pastry for double-crust
   10-inch pie
2 large eggs, lightly beaten
3 cups cooked, mashed pumpkin
1 cup sugar
¼ cup all-purpose flour
1 teaspoon vanilla extract
½ teaspoon salt
½ teaspoon ground allspice
½ teaspoon ground cinnamon
½ teaspoon ground ginger
¼ teaspoon ground cloves
¼ teaspoon ground nutmeg
1 (12-ounce) can evaporated milk
1 cup whipping cream
2 tablespoons honey
2 tablespoons finely chopped
   pecans, toasted

Roll half of pastry to ⅛-inch thickness on a floured surface. Place in a 10-inch pieplate. Roll remaining pastry to ⅛-inch thickness; cut leaf shapes in pastry, making vein markings with back of a knife. Arrange leaves around edge of pieplate, reserving 6 small leaves for garnish. Set aside.

Combine eggs and next 11 ingredients in a large bowl; stir well with a wire whisk. Pour mixture into prepared pastry shell. Bake at 425° for 15 minutes. Reduce heat to 350°; bake 35 to 45 additional minutes or until a knife inserted near center comes out clean. Shield pastry leaves with strips of aluminum foil to prevent excessive browning, if necessary. Remove pie from oven, and let cool.

Place reserved pastry leaves on an ungreased baking sheet. Bake at 450° for 6 to 8 minutes or until browned. Remove to a wire rack; let cool.

Beat whipping cream at high speed of an electric mixer until stiff peaks form; fold in honey. Garnish pie with dollops of sweetened whipped cream. Sprinkle pecans over top. Garnish with small pastry leaves. **Yield:** one 10-inch pie.

Chocolate-coated beans
- Chocolate-covered coffee beans are available at coffee shops, candy counters, or specialty food shops.

Chocolate piecrust

- Crumble piecrust stick into a bowl. Add grated unsweetened chocolate, stirring with a fork to blend.

Unmolding crust

- Carefully invert crust onto a 9-inch pieplate. Remove foil and wax paper; return crust to 10-inch pieplate.

Frozen Mocha Pie

1 commercial piecrust stick
1 (1-ounce) square unsweetened
   chocolate, grated
¾ cup finely chopped pecans
¼ cup firmly packed brown sugar
2 tablespoons cold water
1 teaspoon vanilla extract
½ gallon coffee ice cream,
   softened
1⅓ cups whipping cream

⅓ cup sifted powdered sugar
1 tablespoon instant coffee
   granules
Grated semisweet chocolate
Garnish: chocolate-coated coffee
   beans
½ cup Kahlúa or other
   coffee-flavored liqueur
   (optional)

Crumble piecrust stick into a bowl. Add unsweetened chocolate; stir with a fork. Add pecans and brown sugar, stirring well. Sprinkle water and vanilla over surface; stir until mixture forms a ball.

Line a 10-inch pieplate with aluminum foil; place a circle of wax paper over foil in bottom of pieplate. Press pastry evenly into pieplate. Bake at 375° for 15 minutes; let cool. Carefully invert crust on back of a 9-inch pieplate; remove foil and wax paper. Return crust to 10-inch pieplate. Spoon softened coffee ice cream over prepared crust, spreading evenly; freeze until ice cream is firm.

Beat whipping cream at high speed of electric mixer until foamy; gradually add powdered sugar and coffee granules, beating until stiff peaks form (do not overbeat). Spoon whipped cream mixture on top of frozen pie. Sprinkle with grated semisweet chocolate. Garnish, if desired. Freeze until firm.

Let pie stand at room temperature 5 minutes before serving. Spoon 1 tablespoon Kahlúa over each serving, if desired. **Yield:** one 10-inch pie.

White Chocolate–Banana Cream Pie

1 (13¾-ounce) package coconut macaroons

1 large egg, lightly beaten

1 tablespoon butter or margarine, melted

⅔ cup sugar

¼ cup plus 1 tablespoon cornstarch

⅛ teaspoon salt

3 egg yolks

2 cups milk, divided

1 cup half-and-half

2 (3-ounce) packages white baking bars

3 tablespoons butter or margarine

¾ teaspoon banana flavoring

3 large ripe bananas, thinly sliced

1½ cups whipping cream, divided

1 (3-ounce) package white baking bar

Garnish: white chocolate curls

EQUIPMENT NEEDED:

• Food processor
• 10-inch pieplate
• Heavy saucepan
• Double boiler
• Electric mixer

Position knife blade in food processor bowl. Place macaroons in processor bowl. Cover and pulse 5 or 6 times or until cookies are crumbled. Combine macaroon crumbs, 1 egg, and 1 tablespoon melted butter; stir well. Firmly press crumb mixture over bottom and up sides of a greased 10-inch pieplate. Bake at 350° for 18 to 20 minutes. Let cool.

Combine sugar, cornstarch, and salt in a heavy saucepan. Combine egg yolks, 1½ cups milk, and half-and-half, beating well; gradually stir into sugar mixture.

Heat remaining ½ cup milk and 2 chocolate bars in top of a double boiler over hot water until white chocolate melts. Stir into egg mixture. Cook over medium heat, stirring constantly, until thickened. Remove from heat; add 3 tablespoons butter and banana flavoring. Stir until butter melts. Pour one-third (about 1⅓ cups) of custard mixture into baked crust; top with half of banana slices. Repeat layers, ending with custard. Cover and chill pie several hours.

Heat ¼ cup whipping cream and 1 chocolate bar in top of double boiler until chocolate melts. Let cool. Beat remaining 1¼ cups whipping cream at high speed of an electric mixer until stiff peaks form. Stir 2 tablespoons whipped cream into cooled white chocolate mixture. Gently fold white chocolate mixture into remaining whipped cream; chill. Spread over chilled pie. Garnish, if desired. **Yield:** one 10-inch pie.

Crumbling cookies

• Crumble macaroons in food processor. They'll seem very moist, but will bake into a toasted, golden crust.

Preparing filling

• Stir 2 tablespoons whipped cream into melted and cooled white chocolate to "loosen" it; fold mixture back into remaining whipped cream.

Triple Peanutty Pie

1¼ cups graham cracker crumbs
⅓ cup roasted peanuts, coarsely ground
2 tablespoons sugar
¼ cup plus 2 tablespoons butter or margarine, melted
⅔ cup sugar
3 tablespoons cornstarch
¼ teaspoon salt
2½ cups evaporated milk
2 egg yolks, lightly beaten
½ cup crunchy peanut butter
½ cup peanut butter morsels
1 teaspoon vanilla extract
½ cup whipping cream
1 tablespoon sifted powdered sugar
¼ teaspoon vanilla extract
1 tablespoon chopped roasted peanuts

Combine first 3 ingredients; stir well. Stir in butter. Firmly press crumb mixture evenly over bottom and up sides of a 9-inch pieplate. Bake at 350° for 8 minutes or until browned. Set aside to cool.

Combine ⅔ cup sugar, cornstarch, and salt in a heavy saucepan. Gradually stir in milk. Cook over medium heat, stirring constantly, until thickened and bubbly. Gradually stir about one-fourth of hot mixture into beaten egg yolks; add to remaining hot mixture, stirring constantly. Cook, stirring constantly with a wire whisk, 2 minutes or until thickened and temperature reaches 160°. Remove from heat. Stir in peanut butter, morsels, and 1 teaspoon vanilla. Stir until morsels melt. Pour into prepared crust. Cover and chill pie several hours or until firm.

Beat whipping cream at high speed of electric mixer until foamy; add powdered sugar and ¼ teaspoon vanilla, beating until soft peaks form. Pipe or spoon whipped cream over pie. Sprinkle with chopped peanuts. **Yield:** one 9-inch pie.

Key Lime Tartlets

Cream Cheese Pastry
2 egg yolks
⅓ cup Key lime juice
¾ cup sweetened condensed milk

½ teaspoon grated lime rind
Frozen whipped topping, thawed
Lime wedges

Shape Cream Cheese Pastry dough into 24 balls. Place in ungreased miniature (1¾-inch) muffin pans, shaping each into a shell. Chill 15 minutes. Prick each shell, and bake at 400° for 10 to 12 minutes or until golden. Loosen edges of tart shells from pans, using a sharp knife; do not remove from pans. Let cool completely on wire racks.

Beat egg yolks at medium speed of an electric mixer until thick and lemon colored. Heat Key lime juice over medium heat until hot. Gradually stir about one-fourth of hot lime juice into egg yolks, and add to remaining hot lime juice, stirring constantly. Cook, stirring constantly, 2 minutes. Remove from heat, and let cool. Add milk and lime rind, stirring well.

Spoon filling evenly into baked pastry shells. Chill until ready to serve. Remove tartlets from pans, and top each with whipped topping and lime wedges. **Yield:** 2 dozen.

Cream Cheese Pastry

⅓ cup butter or margarine, softened
1 (3-ounce) package cream cheese, softened

1 cup all-purpose flour

Beat butter and cream cheese at medium speed of an electric mixer until smooth. Add flour, beating well. Wrap dough in wax paper, and chill 2 hours. **Yield:** pastry for 2 dozen 1¾-inch tartlets.

EQUIPMENT NEEDED:
• Miniature 1¾-inch muffin pans
• Wire cooling racks
• Electric mixer
• Small grater
• Saucepan

Pressing dough in pan

• Divide dough into 24 balls. Use your fingertips to press each ball into miniature muffin tins.

Making filling

• Combine egg yolks with hot lime juice to cook the egg yolks; the filling will get very thick when you add sweetened condensed milk.

Little Caramel Pies

Baking shells

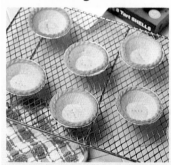

- Bake tart shells according to package directions without the filling. This keeps bottom crusts from getting soggy after filling is added.

Adding caramel

- Add cooled caramel syrup and butter to milk mixture; cook until thickened, stirring constantly with a whisk to prevent lumping.

8 (3-inch) commercial tart shells
⅓ cup sugar
¼ cup boiling water
1½ cups milk
¾ cup sugar
¼ cup cornstarch
3 large eggs, separated

2 tablespoons butter or margarine
1 teaspoon vanilla extract
Pinch of cream of tartar
¼ cup plus 2 tablespoons sugar
¼ teaspoon cornstarch

Bake tart shells according to package directions; let shells cool in tins on wire racks. Sprinkle ⅓ cup sugar in a small heavy skillet; cook over medium heat, stirring constantly, until sugar melts and becomes a light brown syrup. Gradually add boiling water, stirring constantly with a wire whisk. Remove from heat; set aside, and let cool.

Pour milk into a heavy 3-quart saucepan. Cook over medium-high heat, without stirring, until thoroughly heated (do not boil). Combine ¾ cup sugar and ¼ cup cornstarch; stir well. Gradually add cornstarch mixture to egg yolks, beating with a wire whisk until thick. Gradually stir about one-fourth of hot milk into egg yolk mixture; add to remaining hot milk, stirring constantly.

Add cooled caramel syrup and butter to milk mixture; cook over low heat, stirring constantly with a wire whisk, 10 minutes or until mixture is smooth and thickened. Remove from heat; stir in vanilla. Spoon custard into tart shells.

Beat egg whites and cream of tartar at high speed of an electric mixer just until foamy. Combine ¼ cup plus 2 tablespoons sugar and ¼ teaspoon cornstarch; add to egg whites, 1 tablespoon at a time, beating until stiff peaks form and sugar dissolves (2 to 4 minutes). Spread meringue over hot filling, sealing to edge of shells. Bake at 350° for 20 minutes or until golden. Let cool in tins on wire racks. Remove from tins before serving, if desired. **Yield:** eight 3-inch pies.

Flan Ring

1 cup sugar
2 tablespoons water
½ cup slivered almonds
⅔ cup sugar
4 large eggs, lightly beaten

1 (14-ounce) can sweetened
   condensed milk
1¾ cups milk
2 teaspoons vanilla extract

Line a 15- x 10- x 1-inch jellyroll pan with aluminum foil; grease the foil lightly, and set pan aside.

Combine first 3 ingredients in a heavy skillet. Cook over medium heat, stirring constantly with a wooden spoon, until sugar melts and turns golden. Pour mixture quickly onto prepared pan and spread with wooden spoon. Let cool completely. Break candy mixture into pieces; set aside.

Sprinkle ⅔ cup sugar in a large heavy skillet. Cook over medium heat, stirring constantly with a wooden spoon, until sugar melts and turns light brown. Working quickly, pour syrup into a lightly oiled ovenproof 5-cup ring mold, tilting to coat evenly; set aside. (Caramel syrup will harden.)

Combine eggs and remaining 3 ingredients; beat with a wire whisk. Pour custard mixture over syrup in ring mold. Place mold in a large shallow pan. Pour hot water to a depth of 1 inch into large pan. Cover and bake at 350° for 55 to 60 minutes or until a knife inserted near center comes out clean.

Remove mold from water bath, and uncover; let cool on a wire rack. Cover and chill 1 hour, if desired. Loosen edges of flan with a spatula. Invert flan onto a rimmed serving plate; arrange reserved candy pieces in center or around sides of ring. **Yield:** 8 servings.

Doubly caramel
• No, you're not seeing double in this recipe. There are two different steps for making a caramel mixture in a heavy skillet. One becomes a candy brittle topping; the other, a glaze for the flan.

• This flan can also be baked in a lightly oiled 9-inch round cakepan.

Pouring syrup

• Working quickly, pour hot syrup into the oiled ring mold. Tilt mold while syrup is hot to coat bottom evenly. Work carefully—it's hot!

Bread Pudding with Whiskey Sauce

Pouring sauce

• Place each square of bread pudding in an ovenproof dish or bowl. Pour Whiskey Sauce over squares.

1 (1-pound) loaf French bread
2 cups half-and-half
2 cups milk
3 large eggs, lightly beaten
2 cups sugar
½ cup chopped pecans
½ cup raisins
¼ cup shredded or flaked coconut
1 tablespoon plus 1 teaspoon vanilla extract
1½ teaspoons ground cinnamon
½ teaspoon orange extract
2 tablespoons butter or margarine, melted
½ cup shredded or flaked coconut
½ cup chopped pecans
Whiskey Sauce

Break bread into small pieces; place in a shallow bowl. Add half-and-half and milk; let stand 10 minutes. Crush mixture with hands until blended. Add eggs and next 7 ingredients, stirring well.

Pour butter into a 13- x 9- x 2-inch pan; tilt pan to coat evenly. Spoon pudding mixture into pan. Bake at 325° for 40 to 45 minutes or until pudding is very firm. Remove from oven. Let cool.

Combine ½ cup coconut and ½ cup pecans; stir well. Cut pudding into squares. Place each square in a small ovenproof dish. Pour Whiskey Sauce over squares; sprinkle with coconut mixture. Place dishes on a baking sheet. Broil 5½ inches from heat (with electric oven door partially open) until sauce is bubbly and coconut is lightly browned. **Yield:** 15 servings.

Whiskey Sauce

1 cup butter or margarine
2 cups sifted powdered sugar
3 tablespoons bourbon
2 large eggs, lightly beaten

Place butter in top of a double boiler; bring water to a boil. Reduce heat to low; cook until butter melts. Add sugar and bourbon, stirring until sugar dissolves.

Gradually stir about one-fourth of hot mixture into beaten eggs; add to remaining hot mixture in pan, stirring constantly. Cook, stirring constantly, 5 minutes or until mixture thickens. **Yield:** about 2 cups.

Honey-Vanilla Ice Cream

2 cups sugar

⅓ cup all-purpose flour

¼ teaspoon salt

4 cups milk

5 egg yolks, beaten

5 cups half-and-half

1 tablespoon vanilla extract

½ cup honey

Combine first 3 ingredients in a bowl; stir well, and set aside.

Heat milk in a heavy 3-quart saucepan over low heat just until hot. Gradually add sugar mixture to milk, stirring until blended. Cook over medium heat, stirring constantly, 8 minutes or until mixture is smooth and thickened.

Gradually stir about one-fourth of hot mixture into beaten egg yolks; add to remaining hot mixture, stirring constantly. Cook, stirring constantly, 2 minutes. Remove from heat; let cool. Cover; chill custard mixture at least 2 hours.

Add half-and-half and vanilla to chilled custard mixture; stir well to combine. Pour into freezer container of a 1-gallon hand-turned or electric freezer. Freeze according to manufacturer's instructions. Remove dasher, and stir in honey. Pack freezer with additional ice and rock salt, and let stand 1 hour before serving. **Yield:** 3 quarts.

Fresh Peach Ice Cream

3⅓ cups milk
1⅓ cups sugar
¼ cup all-purpose flour
¼ teaspoon salt
3 large eggs, lightly beaten
4 cups peeled, mashed fresh
   peaches

⅔ cup sugar
1⅔ cups half-and-half
1 cup whipping cream
2 teaspoons vanilla extract
1 teaspoon almond extract
Garnish: sliced natural almonds,
   toasted

Heat milk in a 3-quart saucepan over low heat until hot. Combine 1⅓ cups sugar, flour, and salt; gradually add sugar mixture to milk, stirring until blended. Cook mixture over medium heat, stirring constantly, 15 minutes or until thickened.

Gradually stir about one-fourth of hot milk mixture into beaten eggs; add to remaining hot milk mixture, stirring constantly. Cook 1 minute or until temperature reaches 160°; remove from heat, and let cool. Chill at least 2 hours.

Combine mashed peaches and ⅔ cup sugar; stir well. Combine half-and-half and next 3 ingredients in a large bowl; stir well. Add chilled custard mixture, stirring with a wire whisk. Stir in peach mixture. Pour into freezer container of a 1-gallon hand-turned or electric freezer. Freeze according to manufacturer's instructions. Pack freezer with additional ice and rock salt, and let stand 1½ to 2 hours before serving. Garnish each serving, if desired. **Yield:** 3 quarts.

EQUIPMENT NEEDED:

- 3-quart saucepan
- Potato masher or large serving fork
- Wire whisk
- Ice cream freezer and rock salt

Mashing fruit

- Peel and slice fresh peaches. Mash peaches in a large bowl, using a potato masher.

Ripening ice cream

- Pack homemade ice cream (which is very soft by nature) in additional ice and rock salt; let stand 1½ to 2 hours for a firmer consistency.

Toasted Butter Pecan Ice Cream

4 egg yolks, lightly beaten
2 cups sugar
2 cups milk
1 cup whipping cream
2 cups pecan pieces
⅓ cup butter or margarine, melted

¾ teaspoon salt, divided
2 (12-ounce) cans evaporated milk, chilled
1 cup milk
1 tablespoon vanilla extract
1 teaspoon vanilla butter-and-nut flavoring

Combine first 4 ingredients in a large heavy saucepan. Cook over medium-low heat, stirring constantly, until mixture thickens. Remove from heat, and let cool. Chill custard thoroughly.

Spread pecans on a 15- x 10- x 1-inch jellyroll pan. Pour melted butter over pecans, and sprinkle with ½ teaspoon salt. Bake at 325° for 20 to 25 minutes or until pecans are toasted, stirring every 10 minutes. Drain on paper towels.

Add remaining ¼ teaspoon salt, evaporated milk, and remaining 3 ingredients to chilled custard mixture. Pour custard mixture into freezer container of a 1-gallon hand-turned or electric freezer. Add toasted pecan pieces. Freeze according to manufacturer's instructions. Pack freezer with additional ice and rock salt, and let stand at least 1 hour before serving. **Yield:** 2½ quarts.

Mint-Chip Ice Cream Sandwiches

4 quarts mint-chocolate chip ice cream, softened

1 cup shortening

⅔ cup sugar

½ cup firmly packed brown sugar

2 large eggs

1¾ cups all-purpose flour

½ cup cocoa

1 teaspoon baking soda

½ teaspoon salt

1 cup semisweet chocolate mini-morsels

1 teaspoon vanilla extract

Spread each quart of ice cream evenly into a wax paper-lined, 8-inch round cakepan; freeze layers until firm.

Beat shortening at medium speed of an electric mixer until whipped. Gradually add sugars, beating well. Add eggs, one at a time, beating well after each addition. Combine flour and next 3 ingredients; add to creamed mixture. Stir in mini-morsels and vanilla. Chill dough 1 hour.

Shape dough into 32 (1¼-inch) balls; place 3 inches apart on ungreased baking sheets. Flatten each cookie to a 2-inch circle. Bake at 375° for 6 to 8 minutes. (Cookies will spread during baking.) Cool on baking sheets 1 minute. Remove from baking sheets; let cool completely on wire racks.

Remove ice cream from cakepans, and peel off wax paper. Cut ice cream into 3-inch circles, using a 3-inch round cutter. Place each circle between 2 cookies, and press gently. Wrap each sandwich in plastic wrap, and freeze; or serve immediately. **Yield:** 16 sandwiches.

EQUIPMENT NEEDED:

- Four 8-inch cakepans
- Electric mixer
- Baking sheets
- Wire cooling racks
- 3-inch round cutter

Flattening cookies

- Flatten each cookie to a 2-inch circle, using the bottom of a glass. Cookies will spread during baking.

Cutting circles

- Quickly cut circles of ice cream, using a 3-inch cutter. You should get four circles out of each frozen round of ice cream.

Pots de Crème

EQUIPMENT NEEDED:

- Saucepan
- Double boiler
- Wire whisk
- Six 4-ounce ovenproof pots de crème cups or soufflé cups
- 13- x 9- x 2-inch pan
- Wire cooling rack

Pansy garnish

- Edible flowers such as pansies make a lovely garnish on chocolate desserts. Always select nontoxic, pesticide-free flowers.

2 cups half-and-half, divided
½ cup sugar
6 ounces unsweetened chocolate
6 egg yolks
1½ teaspoons vanilla extract
Whipped cream
Garnish: edible flowers

Place 1 cup half-and-half in a small saucepan. Cook over low heat until thoroughly heated, stirring occasionally (do not boil); remove from heat, and stir in sugar. Set aside.

Place remaining 1 cup half-and-half and chocolate in top of a double boiler. Bring water to a boil; reduce heat to low, and cook until chocolate melts and mixture is smooth, stirring occasionally. Remove from heat. Gradually stir hot sugar mixture into hot chocolate mixture, stirring constantly.

Place egg yolks in a large bowl; lightly beat yolks with a wire whisk. Gradually stir about one-fourth of chocolate mixture into yolks; add to remaining chocolate mixture, stirring constantly. Stir in vanilla.

Return mixture to top of double boiler. Cook over low heat, stirring mixture constantly, 3 minutes. Pour mixture evenly into six 4-ounce ovenproof pots de crème cups or soufflé cups, leaving ½-inch headspace. Place in a 13- x 9- x 2-inch pan; add hot water to pan to a depth of 1 inch. Add tops to pots de crème cups, or place a baking sheet on top of soufflé cups. Bake at 325° for 50 minutes to 1 hour or until a knife inserted between center and edge of custard comes out clean (custard should look soft in center).

Uncover and remove cups from pan; place on a wire rack, and let cool to room temperature. Cover and chill thoroughly. Top each serving with a dollop of whipped cream. Garnish, if desired. **Yield:** 6 servings.

Hot Chocolate Soufflé

2 teaspoons sugar
2 tablespoons butter or
   margarine
2 tablespoons all-purpose flour
1 cup half-and-half
2 teaspoons instant coffee
   granules
2 (1-ounce) squares unsweetened
   chocolate

1 (1-ounce) square semisweet
   chocolate
4 large eggs, separated
1 teaspoon vanilla extract
4 egg whites
½ teaspoon cream of tartar
⅔ cup sugar
Vanilla ice cream
Velvet Ganache Sauce

EQUIPMENT NEEDED:

- 2-quart soufflé dish
- String
- Heavy saucepan
- Double boiler
- Electric mixer

Chocolate sauce

- To make sauce, pour hot whipping cream over chocolate morsels. Let stand briefly, and stir until smooth.

Butter bottom of a 2-quart soufflé dish; sprinkle with 2 teaspoons sugar. Cut a piece of aluminum foil long enough to fit around soufflé dish, allowing a 1-inch overlap; fold foil lengthwise into thirds. Oil one side of foil. Wrap foil around outside of dish, oiled side against dish, allowing it to extend 3 inches above rim to form a collar; secure with string. Set aside.

Melt 2 tablespoons butter in a heavy saucepan over low heat; add flour, stirring until smooth. Cook, stirring constantly, 1 minute. Gradually add half-and-half; cook over medium heat, stirring constantly, until thickened and bubbly. Remove from heat. Add coffee granules, stirring to dissolve.

Place chocolates in top of a double boiler; bring water to a boil. Reduce heat to low; cook until chocolates melt. Stir melted chocolate into coffee mixture.

Beat egg yolks. Gradually stir one-fourth of hot mixture into yolks; add to remaining hot mixture, stirring constantly. Add vanilla. Transfer to a large bowl.

Beat 8 egg whites in a large bowl at high speed of an electric mixer until foamy. Add cream of tartar; beat until soft peaks form. Gradually add ⅔ cup sugar, 1 tablespoon at a time, beating until stiff peaks form. Stir 2 tablespoons beaten egg whites into chocolate mixture. Fold remaining egg whites into chocolate mixture, one-third at a time. Spoon mixture into prepared soufflé dish. Make a groove 1½ inches deep around the top in a circle (about 1¼ inches from edge of dish), using a large spoon handle. Bake at 350° for 50 to 60 minutes or until puffed and set. Remove collar. Serve soufflé immediately with ice cream. Drizzle with warm Velvet Ganache Sauce. **Yield:** 8 servings.

Velvet Ganache Sauce

1 cup whipping cream

1 cup semisweet chocolate
   morsels

Bring cream to a simmer in a heavy saucepan. Remove from heat; pour over chocolate morsels. Let stand 1 minute. Stir until chocolate melts. **Yield:** 1½ cups.

Adding crunch

• Remove sauce from heat, and let cool 15 minutes; then stir in evaporated milk for creaminess, and pecans and crushed candy for texture.

Caramel Crunch Sauce

¼ cup butter or margarine
2 tablespoons all-purpose flour
1¼ cups firmly packed brown sugar
¾ cup light corn syrup
1 (5-ounce) can evaporated milk

1½ cups coarsely chopped pecans, toasted
4 (1.4-ounce) English toffee-flavored candy bars, coarsely crushed

Melt butter in a medium saucepan; add flour, stirring until smooth. Stir in brown sugar and corn syrup. Bring mixture to a boil; reduce heat, and simmer, stirring constantly, 5 minutes. Remove from heat, and let cool 15 minutes. Gradually stir in evaporated milk. Stir in pecans and crushed candy. Serve sauce warm over ice cream. **Yield:** 3½ cups.

Piña Colada Sauce

1 tablespoon cornstarch

¼ teaspoon salt

1 (15-ounce) can cream of coconut

⅔ cup milk

2 egg yolks, beaten

2 tablespoons butter or margarine

1 (8-ounce) can crushed pineapple, drained

½ cup flaked coconut

3 tablespoons light rum

Combine cornstarch and salt in a heavy saucepan. Stir in cream of coconut and milk. Cook over medium heat, stirring constantly, until thickened and bubbly. Gradually stir about one-fourth of hot mixture into beaten egg yolks; add to remaining hot mixture, stirring constantly. Cook, stirring constantly, 1 minute or until thickened. Remove from heat. Add butter, stirring until melted. Let cool. Stir in pineapple, coconut, and rum. Cover and chill. Serve sauce over pound cake, gingerbread, or ice cream. **Yield:** 3 cups.

EQUIPMENT NEEDED:

• Heavy saucepan

Make-ahead sauce

• This sauce is served cold so it's a great make-ahead candidate. It'll keep in your refrigerator up to four days.

CLASSIC DIVINITY

SUGAR
COOKIE
CUTOUTS

Cookies &
Candies

LEMON
HEARTS

Backpack Cookies

1 cup butter or margarine, softened
1 cup sugar
1 cup firmly packed brown sugar
2 large eggs
1 teaspoon vanilla extract
2 cups all-purpose flour
½ teaspoon baking powder
1 teaspoon baking soda
⅛ teaspoon salt
2 cups regular oats, uncooked
2 cups oven-toasted rice cereal
1 cup candy-coated milk chocolate pieces
½ cup chopped unsalted roasted peanuts
½ cup chopped pecans
½ cup flaked coconut
1 (6-ounce) package semisweet chocolate morsels

Beat butter at medium speed of an electric mixer until creamy; gradually add sugars, beating until light and fluffy. Add eggs and vanilla; beat well.

Combine flour and next 3 ingredients; add to creamed mixture, mixing well. Fold in oats and remaining ingredients.

Drop dough by rounded tablespoonfuls 2 inches apart onto ungreased baking sheets. Bake at 350° for 10 to 12 minutes or until cookies are lightly browned. Transfer cookies to wire racks, and let cool completely. **Yield:** 7½ dozen.

Triple-Chip Cookies

1 cup butter or margarine, softened
1 cup sugar
½ cup firmly packed brown sugar
2 large eggs
1 teaspoon vanilla extract
2¼ cups all-purpose flour

1 teaspoon baking soda
½ teaspoon salt
¾ cup semisweet chocolate morsels
¾ cup milk chocolate morsels
¾ cup vanilla milk morsels
½ cup chopped blanched almonds

EQUIPMENT NEEDED:
• Electric mixer
• Baking sheets
• Wire cooling racks

Beat butter at medium speed of an electric mixer until creamy; gradually add sugars, beating well. Add eggs and vanilla; beat well.

Combine flour, soda, and salt in a medium bowl. Gradually add flour mixture to creamed mixture, mixing well after each addition. Stir in semisweet chocolate morsels and remaining ingredients.

Drop dough by tablespoonfuls onto ungreased baking sheets. Bake at 350° for 12 to 14 minutes or until lightly browned. Transfer cookies to wire racks, and let cool completely. **Yield:** 4 dozen.

EQUIPMENT NEEDED:
- Electric mixer
- Baking sheets
- Wire cooling racks

Sugar coating

- Roll balls of dough in sugar before baking for a sugary coating.

Chocolate-Ginger Crinkles

⅔ cup shortening
1 cup sugar
1 large egg
¼ cup molasses
2¼ cups all-purpose flour
1½ teaspoons baking soda

½ teaspoon salt
1 tablespoon ground ginger
2 (1-ounce) squares unsweetened chocolate, melted and cooled
Additional sugar

Beat shortening at medium speed of an electric mixer until creamy; gradually add 1 cup sugar, beating well. Add egg, and beat well. Stir in molasses.

Combine flour and next 3 ingredients; stir well. Add to creamed mixture, stirring well. Stir in melted chocolate.

Shape dough into 1-inch balls; roll balls in additional sugar. Place 2 inches apart on lightly greased baking sheets. Bake at 350° for 10 to 12 minutes. Transfer to wire racks, and let cool completely. **Yield:** 4 dozen.

Delicate Lemon Cookies

1⅔ cups all-purpose flour

¼ cup plus 2 tablespoons sifted powdered sugar

¼ teaspoon baking soda

¼ teaspoon cream of tartar

¾ cup finely chopped pecans

1½ teaspoons grated lemon rind

⅔ cup butter or margarine, softened

½ teaspoon lemon extract

Additional powdered sugar

EQUIPMENT NEEDED:
- Baking sheets
- Wire cooling racks
- Sifter

Combine first 6 ingredients in a large bowl; stir well.

Add butter and extract to flour mixture. Knead until mixture is well blended and forms a soft dough.

Shape dough into 32 (1-inch) balls. Place on greased baking sheets. Bake at 325° for 12 to 14 minutes or until barely golden. Let cool slightly.

Transfer cookies to wire racks. Sift powdered sugar over warm cookies, and let cool completely. Roll cookies in additional powdered sugar, if desired. Store cookies in an airtight container. **Yield:** 32 cookies.

Old-Fashioned Peanut Butter Cookies

Designer cookies

- Dip a fork in sugar (so fork won't stick to dough), and flatten cookies in a crisscross pattern.

1 cup butter or margarine, softened	1 tablespoon milk
1 cup creamy peanut butter	2½ cups all-purpose flour
1 cup sugar	2 teaspoons baking soda
1 cup firmly packed brown sugar	¼ teaspoon salt
2 large eggs	1 teaspoon vanilla extract
	Additional sugar

Beat butter and peanut butter at medium speed of an electric mixer until creamy. Gradually add 1 cup sugar and brown sugar to creamed mixture, beating until light and fluffy. Add eggs and milk, beating well.

Combine flour, soda, and salt in a medium bowl; add to creamed mixture, beating well. Stir in vanilla. Cover and chill 2 to 3 hours.

Shape dough into 1¼-inch balls; place 3 inches apart on ungreased baking sheets. Dip a fork in additional sugar, and flatten cookies in a crisscross pattern.

Bake at 375° for 10 minutes. Transfer cookies to wire racks, and let cool completely. **Yield:** 6 dozen.

Cinnamon-Pecan Icebox Cookies

1 cup butter or margarine,
    softened
¾ cup sugar
¼ cup firmly packed brown
    sugar
1 large egg
1 teaspoon vanilla extract

2¼ cups all-purpose flour
1½ teaspoons baking powder
½ teaspoon salt
1 cup finely chopped pecans
¼ cup sugar
1½ teaspoons ground cinnamon

Beat butter at medium speed of an electric mixer until creamy; gradually add ¾ cup sugar and brown sugar, beating well. Add egg and vanilla, beating well.

  Combine flour, baking powder, and salt; add to creamed mixture, beating well at medium speed. Stir in pecans. Cover and chill dough 2 hours.

  Shape dough into 2 (6- x 2½-inch) rolls. Wrap rolls in wax paper, and freeze until firm.

  Combine ¼ cup sugar and cinnamon; stir well. Unwrap dough, and roll in sugar mixture. Slice frozen dough into ¼-inch-thick slices; place on ungreased baking sheets.

  Bake at 350° for 12 to 14 minutes or until lightly browned. Transfer cookies to wire racks, and let cool completely. **Yield:** 4 dozen.

EQUIPMENT NEEDED:
- Electric mixer
- Baking sheets
- Wire cooling racks

Freezing dough

- You can freeze this cookie dough up to three months. Freeze it in rolls, so you can slice and bake a few at a time.

Sugar Cookie Cutouts

EQUIPMENT NEEDED:
- Electric mixer
- Rolling pin
- 3-inch cookie cutter
- Baking sheets
- Wire cooling rack

Colored sugar

• Decorator sugar comes in many colors and is easy to find on the baking aisle in the grocery store.

½ cup unsalted butter, softened
1 cup sugar
1 large egg
1 teaspoon grated lemon rind
1 tablespoon lemon juice
2 cups all-purpose flour
2 teaspoons baking powder
¼ teaspoon salt
Decorator sugar

Beat butter at medium speed of an electric mixer until creamy; gradually add 1 cup sugar, beating until light and fluffy. Add egg, beating well. Add grated lemon rind and lemon juice, beating until blended.

Combine flour, baking powder, and salt; add to creamed mixture, beating well. Shape into a ball; wrap in wax paper, and chill at least 8 hours.

Divide dough into 3 equal portions. Work with 1 portion of dough at a time, storing remainder in refrigerator. Roll dough to ⅛-inch thickness on a lightly floured surface.

Cut with a 3-inch cookie cutter, and place 2 inches apart on lightly greased baking sheets. Sprinkle cookies with decorator sugar. Repeat procedure with remaining dough.

Bake at 375° for 10 to 12 minutes or until edges of cookies are lightly browned. Transfer cookies to a wire rack, and let cool completely. **Yield:** 20 cookies.

EQUIPMENT NEEDED:
- Electric mixer
- Baking sheet
- Wide-blade spatula
- Muffin pans or custard cups

Paper fortunes
- Create your own paper fortunes to insert into these cookies. Pick your favorite proverbs, or write predictions for a new year.

Shaping and baking

- Spoon batter onto well-greased baking sheet; spread to a 3 or 3½-inch circle.

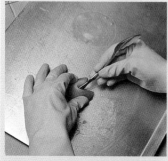

- Place a fortune in center of cookie, and use a spoon handle to help fold and shape each cookie. Wearing gloves protects tender hands from hot cookies.

Almond Fortune Cookies

½ cup all-purpose flour	½ teaspoon lemon extract
¼ cup sugar	2 egg whites
1 tablespoon cornstarch	2 tablespoons ground blanched
Dash of salt	almonds
¼ cup vegetable oil	18 paper fortunes (2½- x
¾ teaspoon vanilla extract	½-inch)

Combine first 4 ingredients in a medium mixing bowl; stir well. Add oil and next 3 ingredients, beating well at medium speed of an electric mixer until smooth. Stir in almonds.

Spoon 1 heaping teaspoonful batter onto a well-greased baking sheet; spread batter to a 3- to 3½-inch circle with back of a spoon. Bake 2 cookies at a time at 325° for 8 to 9 minutes or until golden. (Let baking sheet cool completely between batches, and regrease baking sheet each time.)

Working quickly, remove 1 cookie at a time with a wide spatula. Place a paper fortune in center of each cookie; fold cookie in half. Using the handle of a spoon, indent each cookie in the middle of the fold, pulling the ends of the cookie towards the center (see photo). Place each cookie in an ungreased muffin cup to hold its shape while cooling. (If cookie cools before it is formed, reheat in oven about 1 minute.) Let cool completely. Store in an airtight container. **Yield:** 1½ dozen.

Buttery Lace Cookies

½ cup firmly packed brown
   sugar

⅓ cup butter

2 tablespoons whipping cream

¾ cup minced almonds, pecans,
   or unsalted peanuts

3 tablespoons all-purpose flour

EQUIPMENT NEEDED:

- Saucepan
- Baking sheets
- Metal spatula
- Wooden spoons
- Wire cooling racks

Rolling cookies

• When cookies are cool
enough to touch, quickly lift
them with a metal spatula, flip
them, and roll each cookie
around the handle of a
wooden spoon. Let cool.

Combine first 3 ingredients in a saucepan. Bring to a boil over medium heat, stirring often. Remove from heat; stir in nuts and flour.

Spoon batter by tablespoonfuls 3 inches apart onto aluminum foil-lined or parchment paper-lined baking sheets, making 3 cookies at a time. Spread batter into circles.

Bake at 350° for 6 to 8 minutes or until edges are lightly browned. (Cookies will spread during baking.) Remove from oven, and let cool slightly (about 1 minute).

When cookies hold their shape and are cool enough to touch, quickly lift them with a metal spatula. Flip cookies, and roll each around the handle of a wooden spoon or another cylindrical object. Let cool completely on wire racks. (If baked cookies become too crisp to roll, reheat for 30 seconds.) When cookies have cooled, carefully remove wooden spoons. Repeat with remaining batter, making 3 cookies at a time. Store cooled cookies in an airtight container up to one week. **Yield:** 1½ dozen.

Variation: Fill cooled cookies with whipped cream. Or, dip ends of cooled cookies in 1 cup melted semisweet chocolate morsels; let harden on wax paper.

Almond Cream Bars

½ cup butter or margarine
¼ cup sugar
2 tablespoons cocoa
2 teaspoons vanilla extract
¼ teaspoon salt
1 large egg, lightly beaten
1¾ cups vanilla wafer crumbs
1 cup slivered almonds, toasted and chopped

½ cup flaked coconut
Creamy Frosting
2 (1-ounce) squares semisweet chocolate
1 tablespoon butter or margarine
¼ cup sliced almonds, toasted

Combine first 6 ingredients in a heavy saucepan; cook over low heat, stirring constantly, until butter melts and mixture begins to thicken. Remove from heat; stir in wafer crumbs, chopped almonds, and coconut. Press mixture firmly into an ungreased 9-inch square pan. Cover and chill.

Spread Creamy Frosting over chilled almond mixture; cover and chill thoroughly. Melt semisweet chocolate and 1 tablespoon butter in a small heavy saucepan over low heat, stirring often. Remove from heat, and let cool. Spoon melted chocolate mixture into a heavy-duty, zip-top plastic bag or a decorating bag fitted with a No. 2 round tip; seal plastic bag. Snip a tiny hole in one corner of zip-top bag, using scissors.

Cut chilled mixture into 16 bars. Remove bars from pan. Pipe chocolate mixture in a decorative design over bars. Top each bar with toasted almond slices. **Yield:** 16 bars.

Creamy Frosting

⅓ cup butter or margarine, softened
3 tablespoons whipping cream

½ teaspoon almond extract
2½ to 3 cups sifted powdered sugar

Beat butter at high speed of an electric mixer until creamy. Add whipping cream and almond extract; beat just until blended. Gradually add powdered sugar, beating until frosting is spreading consistency. **Yield:** 1½ cups.

Frosted Blonde Brownies

⅔ cup butter or margarine
1 cup firmly packed brown sugar
1½ cups all-purpose flour
1 teaspoon baking powder
½ teaspoon salt
¾ teaspoon ground cinnamon
2 large eggs

1 (7.5-ounce) package almond
  brickle chips
1 cup chopped pecans, lightly
  toasted
1 tablespoon vanilla extract
Brown Sugar Frosting

Line an 11- x 7- x 1½-inch baking dish with a large sheet of aluminum foil, allowing foil to extend 1 inch beyond ends of dish. Butter foil, and set aside.

Melt ⅔ cup butter and brown sugar in a large skillet over medium heat. Cook until golden and bubbly (about 5 minutes), stirring often. Remove from heat, and transfer to a large mixing bowl. Combine flour and next 3 ingredients; stir well. Add flour mixture to sugar mixture. Beat at medium speed of an electric mixer until blended. Add eggs, beating well.

Stir in brickle chips, pecans, and vanilla. Spread batter in foil-lined pan. Bake at 350° for 25 to 30 minutes. Let cool completely in pan. Frost with Brown Sugar Frosting. Let stand at least 30 minutes. Carefully lift foil out of pan. Cut into bars, using a sharp knife. **Yield:** 1½ dozen.

Brown Sugar Frosting

¼ cup butter or margarine
1 cup firmly packed brown sugar
¼ cup evaporated milk

1 tablespoon light corn syrup
¼ teaspoon salt
2 teaspoons vanilla extract

Combine first 4 ingredients in a heavy saucepan. Bring mixture to a boil over medium heat; boil 4 minutes. Remove sugar mixture from heat. Pour into a mixing bowl, and let cool completely. Add salt and vanilla, and beat at medium-high speed of an electric mixer 3 to 4 minutes or until frosting is spreading consistency. **Yield:** 1 cup.

★★★★★

EQUIPMENT NEEDED:
• 11- x 7- x 1½-inch baking dish
• Skillet
• Electric mixer
• Heavy saucepan

Foil lining

• Line baking dish with a large sheet of aluminum foil. This makes it easy to remove baked uncut brownies from the pan.

Lemon Hearts

2 cups all-purpose flour
½ cup sifted powdered sugar
1 cup butter or margarine, softened
1 teaspoon vanilla extract
2 cups sugar
2 tablespoons cornstarch
5 large eggs, lightly beaten

1 tablespoon grated lemon rind
¼ cup plus 2 tablespoons lemon juice
2 tablespoons butter or margarine, melted
2 to 4 tablespoons powdered sugar
Garnish: lemon rind knots

Combine first 4 ingredients; beat at medium speed of an electric mixer until blended. Pat mixture into a greased 13- x 9- x 2-inch baking dish. Bake at 350° for 18 minutes or until golden.

   Combine 2 cups sugar and cornstarch. Add eggs and next 3 ingredients; beat well. Pour mixture over crust.

   Bake at 350° for 20 to 25 minutes or until set. Let cool. Chill well. Sift 2 to 4 tablespoons powdered sugar over top, and cut into hearts or bars. Garnish, if desired. **Yield:** 14 hearts or 2½ dozen bars.

EQUIPMENT NEEDED:

- Electric mixer
- 13- x 9- x 2-inch baking dish
- Sifter
- Heart-shaped cutter (optional)

Cutting hearts

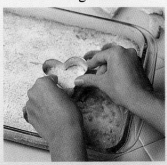

- To cut Lemon Hearts, dip a heart-shaped cutter in powdered sugar, and press down into uncut dish of lemon bars.

Chocolate-Peanut Butter Fudge

2½ cups sugar
¼ cup cocoa
1 cup milk
1 tablespoon light corn syrup
½ cup butter or margarine, divided

1 cup chopped pecans
½ cup peanut butter
2 teaspoons vanilla extract

Combine first 4 ingredients in a Dutch oven. Cook over medium heat, stirring constantly, until sugar dissolves. Add 2 tablespoons butter; stir until butter melts. Cover and boil 3 minutes. Uncover and continue to cook, without stirring, until mixture reaches soft ball stage (234°).

   Remove mixture from heat, and, without stirring, add remaining ¼ cup plus 2 tablespoons butter, pecans, peanut butter, and vanilla. Let cool 10 minutes.

   Beat mixture until well blended; pour immediately into a buttered 9-inch square pan. Let cool; cut fudge into 1½-inch squares. **Yield:** 3 dozen.

Double-Treat Toffee

2 cups sugar
1 cup butter or margarine
¼ cup water
1 teaspoon vanilla extract

2½ cups semisweet chocolate
   morsels, divided
2 cups finely chopped pecans,
   toasted and divided

Combine first 3 ingredients in a 3-quart saucepan. Cook over low heat, stirring gently, until sugar dissolves. Cover and cook over medium heat 2 to 3 minutes to wash down sugar crystals from sides of pan. Uncover and cook to hard crack stage (300°). Remove from heat, and stir in vanilla. Pour into a greased 15- x 10- x 1-inch jellyroll pan, quickly spreading mixture to edges of pan.

  Sprinkle 1¼ cups chocolate morsels over hot toffee; let stand 1 minute or until chocolate begins to melt. Spread chocolate evenly over candy. Sprinkle with 1 cup chopped pecans. Let candy stand until set.

  Place remaining 1¼ cups chocolate morsels in top of a double boiler; bring water to a boil. Reduce heat to low, and cook until chocolate melts. Remove from heat. Run a knife around edge of toffee in jellyroll pan. Carefully invert toffee onto a wax paper-lined baking sheet. Spread melted chocolate over uncoated side of toffee. Sprinkle with remaining 1 cup chopped pecans. Let stand until set. Break toffee into pieces. Store in an airtight container. **Yield:** 2 pounds.

EQUIPMENT NEEDED:

- 3-quart saucepan
- Clip-on candy thermometer
- 15- x 10- x 1-inch jellyroll pan
- Double boiler
- Baking sheet

Spreading chocolate

- Sprinkle chocolate morsels over hot toffee, and let stand 1 minute to soften; then spread chocolate evenly over candy.

★★★★★

EQUIPMENT NEEDED:
- 3-quart saucepan
- Clip-on candy thermometer
- Electric mixer

Sunny-day divinity
- You'll have the best results if you make divinity on a sunny day. Humid weather can lead to sticky candy.

Cooking sugar

- Cook the sugar mixture to 260°. Don't let clip-on thermometer touch the bottom of saucepan, or it may not record accurate temperature.

Classic Divinity

2½ cups sugar
½ cup water
½ cup light corn syrup

2 egg whites
1 teaspoon vanilla extract
1 cup chopped pecans, toasted

Combine first 3 ingredients in a 3-quart saucepan; cook over low heat, stirring constantly, until sugar dissolves. Cover and cook over medium heat 2 to 3 minutes to wash down sugar crystals from sides of pan. Uncover and cook over medium heat, without stirring, to hard ball stage (260°). Remove from heat.

   Beat egg whites in a large mixing bowl at high speed of an electric mixer until stiff peaks form. Pour hot sugar mixture in a heavy stream over beaten egg whites while beating constantly at high speed. Add vanilla, and continue beating just until mixture holds its shape (3 to 4 minutes). Stir in pecans.

   Drop by rounded teaspoonfuls onto wax paper. Let cool. **Yield:** 1½ pounds.

Variations: For Cherry Divinity, substitute 1 cup finely chopped red candied cherries for pecans. For Pink Divinity, add 4 to 5 drops of red food coloring with vanilla extract.

Peanut Brittle

2 cups sugar
1 cup light corn syrup
¾ cup water
2 cups raw peanuts
3 tablespoons butter or
   margarine

1 teaspoon vanilla extract
1 teaspoon baking soda
¼ teaspoon salt

Combine first 3 ingredients in a 3-quart saucepan. Cook over medium-low heat, stirring constantly, until sugar dissolves. Cover mixture, and cook over medium heat 2 to 3 minutes to wash down sugar crystals from sides of pan. Add peanuts; cook until mixture reaches hard crack stage (300°), stirring occasionally. Remove from heat. Stir in butter and remaining ingredients.

   Working quickly, pour candy mixture into a buttered 15- x 10- x 1-inch jellyroll pan; spread to edges of pan. Let cool completely; break into pieces. Store in an airtight container. **Yield:** about 2 pounds.

EQUIPMENT NEEDED:

• 3-quart saucepan
• Clip-on candy thermometer
• 15- x 10- x 1-inch jellyroll
  pan

Pouring brittle

• Working quickly, pour candy mixture into buttered pan, and spread to edges of pan before candy hardens.

TEXAS BRUNCH

VEGETABLE MEDLEY
FRITTATA

Eggs & Cheese

DELUXE MACARONI AND CHEESE

Baked Eggs in Spinach Cups

EQUIPMENT NEEDED:
- Grater
- Heavy saucepan
- Four 6-ounce custard cups
- Baking sheet (optional)

Spinach cups

- Spoon spinach mixture into each custard cup, spreading sides high enough to contain the egg.

- Break an egg into each spinach cup. Cover and bake until set.

1 (10-ounce) package frozen chopped spinach
2 tablespoons butter or margarine
2 tablespoons finely chopped onion
2 tablespoons all-purpose flour
1 teaspoon chicken-flavored bouillon granules
1 cup milk
¼ teaspoon salt
⅛ teaspoon ground nutmeg
1 (2-ounce) jar diced pimiento, drained
4 large eggs
½ cup (2 ounces) shredded Cheddar cheese
Grated Parmesan cheese
3 slices bacon, cooked and crumbled

Cook spinach according to package directions. Drain; press between paper towels to remove excess moisture. Set spinach aside.

Melt butter in a heavy saucepan over low heat; add onion, and cook until onion is tender. Stir in flour and bouillon granules; cook, stirring constantly, 1 minute. Gradually add milk; cook over medium heat, stirring constantly, until mixture is thickened and bubbly. Stir in salt, nutmeg, and pimiento. Add reserved spinach, stirring well.

Spoon spinach mixture into four 6-ounce custard cups, spreading up sides of cups. Break 1 egg into each cup. Place cups on a baking sheet, if desired. Cover loosely with foil.

Bake at 350° for 25 to 30 minutes or until eggs are set. Remove foil. Sprinkle with cheeses and bacon; bake, uncovered, 3 to 5 additional minutes or until cheeses melt. **Yield:** 4 servings.

Breakfast Pizza

6 small new potatoes
1 (8-ounce) package refrigerated
    crescent dinner rolls
1 medium-size green pepper,
    seeded and chopped
½ teaspoon dried oregano
1 (6-ounce) package Canadian
    bacon, coarsely chopped
1 tablespoon butter or
    margarine, melted

1 cup (4 ounces) shredded
    Gouda cheese, divided
1 cup (4 ounces) shredded colby-
    Monterey Jack cheese blend,
    divided
5 large eggs, lightly beaten
½ cup milk
¼ teaspoon pepper

EQUIPMENT NEEDED:

• Grater
• Saucepan
• 12-inch pizza pan or other
  large round pan
• Skillet

Forming one crust

• Separate crescent dough into triangles. Place triangles in greased pizza pan, pressing together to form crust and rim.

Cook potatoes in boiling water 10 to 15 minutes or until tender. Let cool slightly; peel skins. Slice potatoes into ¼-inch slices. Set aside.

Separate crescent dough into 8 triangles; place triangles with elongated points toward center in a lightly greased 12-inch pizza pan. Press bottom and sides to form a crust and rim. Seal perforations. Bake at 375° for 5 to 6 minutes. Remove from oven. (Crust will be puffy when removed from oven.) Reduce oven temperature to 350°.

Cook green pepper, oregano, and Canadian bacon in butter in a large skillet over medium-high heat, stirring constantly, 2 minutes. Arrange half of mixture on crust. Top with reserved potato slices. Sprinkle with ½ cup of each cheese. Combine eggs, milk, and ¼ teaspoon pepper; stir well. Pour over pizza. Sprinkle with remaining meat mixture and remaining cheese. Bake, uncovered, at 350° for 30 minutes. **Yield:** 6 servings.

Hearty Cheese Omelet

Cooking the omelet

• As the egg mixture starts to cook, lift edges of omelet with a spatula, and tilt pan so uncooked portion flows underneath.

6 slices bacon
2 tablespoons chopped onion
2 tablespoons diced green pepper
2 tablespoons diced sweet red pepper
½ cup peeled, diced potato
6 large eggs
2 tablespoons water
¼ teaspoon salt
Dash of ground white pepper
½ cup (2 ounces) finely shredded Cheddar cheese, divided
Garnishes: tomato wedges, fresh parsley sprigs

Cook bacon in a 10-inch skillet until crisp; remove bacon, reserving 2 tablespoons drippings in skillet. Crumble bacon, and set aside.

Cook onion and diced peppers in drippings over medium-high heat, stirring constantly, until tender; add potato, and cook until browned. Remove vegetables with a slotted spoon; set aside, and keep warm.

Combine eggs and next 3 ingredients in a bowl; whisk just until blended. Pour egg mixture into hot skillet over medium heat. As mixture starts to cook, gently lift edges of omelet with a spatula, and tilt pan so uncooked portion of egg flows underneath.

Sprinkle half of omelet with reserved vegetable mixture, three-fourths of shredded cheese, and all but 1 tablespoon crumbled bacon. Fold omelet in half, and transfer to a serving plate. Sprinkle omelet with reserved 1 tablespoon crumbled bacon and remaining one-fourth of shredded cheese. Garnish, if desired. **Yield:** 1 to 2 servings.

Ultimate Scrambled Eggs

1 (3-ounce) package cream
   cheese, softened
5 large eggs, divided
¼ cup milk
½ teaspoon cracked pepper
⅛ teaspoon salt
2 tablespoons chopped fresh
   chives

1 tablespoon butter or margarine
½ cup (2 ounces) shredded
   Monterey Jack cheese
3 slices bacon, cooked and
   coarsely crumbled

Beat cream cheese at medium speed of an electric mixer until smooth. Add 2 eggs; beat until smooth. Add remaining 3 eggs, milk, pepper, and salt; beat until blended. Stir in chives.

   Melt butter in a large nonstick skillet. Add egg mixture; cook over medium-low heat, without stirring, until egg mixture begins to set on bottom. Draw a rubber spatula across bottom of skillet to form large curds. Add shredded cheese and bacon. Continue cooking until cheese melts and eggs are firm but still moist (do not stir constantly). Serve immediately. **Yield:** 3 to 4 servings.

EQUIPMENT NEEDED:
- Grater
- Electric mixer
- Large nonstick skillet
- Spatula

Cheese choices
- Monterey Jack with jalapeño peppers, colby-Jack, or sharp Cheddar are good options if you want to vary the cheese in this recipe.

Scrambling eggs

- When the egg mixture begins to set in the skillet, draw spatula across bottom of skillet to form large curds of egg.

Texas Brunch

3 tablespoons butter or margarine
3 tablespoons all-purpose flour
2 cups milk
2 cups (8 ounces) shredded Cheddar cheese, divided
6 hard-cooked eggs, chopped
½ cup mayonnaise
¼ teaspoon salt
¼ teaspoon hot sauce
⅛ teaspoon pepper
Quick Cornbread
8 slices bacon, cooked and crumbled
⅓ cup chopped green onions

Melt butter in a large saucepan over low heat; add flour, stirring until smooth. Cook, stirring constantly, 1 minute. Gradually add milk, and cook over medium heat, stirring constantly, until thickened and bubbly. Stir in ¾ cup shredded cheese and next 5 ingredients. Cook, stirring constantly, until cheese melts.

   Cut Quick Cornbread into 6 pieces; remove from pan, and split each piece in half horizontally. Place 2 pieces each, cut sides up, on individual serving plates. Spoon egg mixture evenly over sliced cornbread. Top evenly with remaining 1¼ cups shredded cheese. Sprinkle with crumbled bacon and chopped green onions. **Yield:** 6 servings.

Quick Cornbread

⅔ cup yellow cornmeal
⅔ cup all-purpose flour
1 tablespoon sugar
1 teaspoon baking powder
½ teaspoon baking soda
½ teaspoon salt
¼ teaspoon ground red pepper
1 large egg, lightly beaten
2 tablespoons shortening, melted
2 tablespoons milk
1 (8-ounce) carton sour cream

Combine first 7 ingredients in a medium bowl; stir well. Make a well in center of mixture. Combine egg and remaining 3 ingredients; add to dry ingredients, stirring just until moistened. Spoon batter into a greased 8-inch square pan. Bake at 425° for 15 minutes or until golden. **Yield:** 6 servings.

Huevos Rancheros

6 (6-inch) corn tortillas
Vegetable oil
1 cup chopped green pepper
1 cup chopped onion
2 cloves garlic, minced
2 tablespoons olive oil
2 (16-ounce) cans whole
    tomatoes, drained and
    chopped
1 (4.5-ounce) can chopped green
    chiles

2 teaspoons chili powder
½ teaspoon ground cumin
¼ teaspoon salt
¼ teaspoon pepper
6 large eggs
1 cup (4 ounces) shredded
    Cheddar cheese
¼ cup sliced ripe olives
Garnish: hot peppers

EQUIPMENT NEEDED:

• Grater
• Skillet
• Tongs or long-handled fork
• 11- x 7- x 1½-inch
  baking dish

Fry tortillas, one at a time, in ¼ cup hot vegetable oil in a skillet 3 to 5 seconds on each side or just until softened, adding additional oil, if necessary. Drain tortillas thoroughly on paper towels. Immediately line an 11- x 7- x 1½-inch baking dish with tortillas, letting tortillas extend up sides of dish. Set dish aside.

Cook green pepper, onion, and garlic in olive oil over medium-high heat, stirring constantly, until tender. Add chopped tomato and next 5 ingredients. Cover and simmer 3 minutes or until thickened.

Pour tomato mixture over tortillas. Make 6 indentations in tomato mixture; break 1 egg into each indentation.

Cover and bake at 350° for 25 minutes or just until eggs are set. Sprinkle with Cheddar cheese and olives. Bake, uncovered, 5 additional minutes or until cheese melts. Garnish, if desired. Serve immediately. **Yield:** 6 servings.

Softening tortillas

• Fry tortillas in hot oil just until softened. This makes them pliable and easy to fit in the baking dish.

Adding eggs

• Break an egg into each indentation of tomato mixture. The indentations hold eggs in place during baking.

EQUIPMENT NEEDED:
- 8- or 10-inch ovenproof skillet (such as cast-iron)
- Electric mixer or wire whisk

Frittata fact
- Frittatas are typically cooked over the stovetop first and then finished under a broiler.

Cheese topping

- Sprinkle frittata with Parmesan; then broil until golden.

Vegetable Medley Frittata

3 tablespoons butter or margarine	1 small zucchini, thinly sliced
1 cup sliced fresh mushrooms	8 large eggs
3 tablespoons diagonally sliced green onions	½ teaspoon salt
2 tablespoons diced sweet red pepper	¼ teaspoon pepper
5 fresh asparagus spears, cut into 1½-inch pieces	1½ tablespoons butter or margarine
	3 tablespoons grated Parmesan cheese

Melt 3 tablespoons butter in a large skillet over medium-high heat. Add mushrooms and next 4 ingredients; cook, stirring constantly, until tender. Drain vegetable mixture on paper towels, and set aside.

Combine eggs, salt, and pepper in a large bowl; beat until frothy. Add vegetable mixture, stirring gently.

Melt 1½ tablespoons butter in an 8- or 10-inch ovenproof skillet. Pour egg mixture into skillet; cover and cook over medium-low heat 7 to 9 minutes or until eggs are set and a slight crust forms on bottom of frittata. Remove from heat; sprinkle with Parmesan cheese. Broil frittata 5½ inches from heat (with electric oven door partially opened) 2 to 3 minutes or until golden. Cut into wedges, and serve immediately. **Yield:** 6 servings.

Wine and Cheese Strata

1 (1-pound) loaf French bread
1 (8-ounce) package fresh
   mushrooms, sliced
1½ teaspoons chopped fresh
   oregano or ½ teaspoon dried
   oregano
¼ teaspoon pepper
¼ cup butter or margarine,
   melted
⅔ cup dry white wine (or milk)
2 cups chopped cooked ham
1 cup (4 ounces) shredded Swiss
   cheese

1 cup (4 ounces) shredded
   Monterey Jack cheese
½ cup chopped green onions
6 large eggs
2 cups milk
¼ cup spicy brown mustard
¼ teaspoon pepper
Hot sauce to taste
1⅓ cups sour cream
¾ cup grated Parmesan cheese
Garnishes: fresh oregano sprigs,
   fresh mushroom slices

Cut off and discard crusty ends of bread. Tear rest of loaf into bite-size chunks. Arrange bread in a heavily greased 13- x 9- x 2-inch baking dish. Set aside.

Cook mushrooms, 1½ teaspoons fresh oregano, and ¼ teaspoon pepper in butter in a large skillet over medium-high heat, stirring constantly, until mushrooms are tender. Sprinkle mushroom mixture over bread. Pour white wine over mushroom mixture. Sprinkle with ham and next 3 ingredients.

Combine eggs and next 4 ingredients. Beat with a wire whisk until blended. Pour egg mixture over layers in dish. Cover and chill 8 hours.

Bake strata, covered, at 350° for 45 to 50 minutes. Remove from oven, and spread with sour cream. Sprinkle with Parmesan cheese. Broil 4 inches from heat (with electric oven door partially opened) 2 to 3 minutes or until lightly browned. Garnish, if desired. Serve hot. **Yield:** 8 servings.

EQUIPMENT NEEDED:
• Grater
• 13- x 9- x 2-inch baking
  dish
• Large skillet
• Wire whisk

Wine substitution
• If you'd like to omit the wine in this rich brunch dish, substitute ⅔ cup milk.

Tearing bread

• Tear French bread into bite-size chunks, and arrange snugly in dish.

Soaking bread

• Pour egg mixture over layers in dish. The egg mixture will soak into the bread overnight.

Favorite Cheese Blintzes

EQUIPMENT NEEDED:

- Electric mixer
- Skillet
- 6 or 7-inch crêpe pan or small heavy skillet

Cooking crêpes

- To make crêpes, pour 2 tablespoons batter into pan; quickly tilt pan in all directions so batter coats it with a thin film.

1 cup large-curd cottage cheese
½ (8-ounce) package cream cheese, softened
3 tablespoons sugar
1 tablespoon milk
1 teaspoon grated lemon rind
1 teaspoon vanilla extract
Crêpes
1 tablespoon butter or margarine
Sour cream
Strawberry preserves
Garnish: fresh strawberries

Combine cottage cheese and cream cheese; beat at medium speed of an electric mixer until smooth. Add sugar and next 3 ingredients; stir well. Cover and chill 20 minutes.

Spoon 3 tablespoons cheese filling in center of each Crêpe. Fold right and left sides over filling; fold bottom and top of Crêpe over filling, forming a square.

Melt butter in a large skillet. Place blintzes in skillet, seam side down. Cook over medium heat until lightly browned, turning once. Serve with sour cream and preserves. Garnish, if desired. **Yield:** 4 servings.

Crêpes

½ cup all-purpose flour
¼ teaspoon salt
⅔ cup milk
1 large egg
2 tablespoons butter or margarine, melted
Vegetable oil

Combine first 3 ingredients, beating at low speed of an electric mixer until smooth. Add egg, and beat well; stir in butter. Refrigerate batter 1 hour. (This allows flour particles to swell and soften so that crêpes will be light in texture.)

Brush bottom of a 6- or 7-inch crêpe pan or heavy skillet with oil; place pan over medium heat just until hot but not smoking. Pour 2 tablespoons batter into pan; quickly tilt pan in all directions so batter covers pan with a thin film. Cook about 1 minute.

Lift edge of crêpe to test for doneness. Crêpe is ready for flipping when it can be shaken loose from pan. Flip crêpe, and cook about 30 seconds on other side. (This side of the crêpe is usually spotty brown and is the side on which the filling is placed.)

Place crêpes on a towel, and allow to cool. Repeat procedure until all batter is used. Stack crêpes between layers of wax paper to prevent sticking. **Yield:** eight 6-inch crêpes.

Caramel-Soaked French Toast

EQUIPMENT NEEDED:
- Saucepan
- 13- x 9- x 2-inch baking dish

Arranging bread

- Arrange bread slices over syrup mixture in dish, packing them tightly.

Cinnamon topping

- After bread has soaked up the egg mixture, sprinkle with cinnamon-sugar, and drizzle with melted butter.

1½ cups firmly packed brown sugar

¾ cup butter or margarine

¼ cup plus 2 tablespoons light corn syrup

10 (1¾-inch-thick) slices French bread

4 large eggs, lightly beaten

2½ cups milk or half-and-half

1 tablespoon vanilla extract

¼ teaspoon salt

3 tablespoons sugar

1½ teaspoons ground cinnamon

¼ cup butter or margarine, melted

Combine first 3 ingredients in a medium saucepan. Cook over medium heat, stirring constantly, 5 minutes or until mixture is bubbly. Pour syrup mixture evenly into a lightly greased 13- x 9- x 2-inch baking dish. Arrange bread slices over syrup.

Combine eggs and next 3 ingredients; stir well. Gradually pour mixture over bread slices. Cover and chill at least 8 hours.

Combine 3 tablespoons sugar and cinnamon; stir well. Sprinkle evenly over soaked bread. Drizzle ¼ cup melted butter over bread. Bake, uncovered, at 350° for 45 to 50 minutes or until golden and bubbly. Serve immediately. **Yield:** 10 servings.

Deluxe Macaroni and Cheese

1 (8-ounce) package elbow
    macaroni
2 cups (8 ounces) shredded
    Cheddar cheese
2 cups cottage cheese
1 cup diced cooked ham
3 tablespoons finely chopped
    onion
¼ teaspoon salt

¼ teaspoon pepper
1 (8-ounce) carton sour cream
1 large egg, lightly beaten
1 cup soft breadcrumbs
2 tablespoons butter or
    margarine, melted
¼ teaspoon paprika
Garnishes: sliced cherry
    tomatoes, fresh parsley

EQUIPMENT NEEDED:
• Grater
• 2-quart casserole

Cook macaroni according to package directions; drain well.

Place macaroni, Cheddar cheese, and next 7 ingredients in a large bowl; stir gently to combine. Spoon into a lightly greased 2-quart casserole.

Combine soft breadcrumbs, melted butter, and paprika in a small bowl, stirring well. Sprinkle breadcrumb mixture diagonally across top of casserole, forming stripes. Bake, uncovered, at 350° for 30 to 40 minutes or until topping is golden. Garnish, if desired. **Yield:** 6 servings.

Fresh Corn Custard

2 tablespoons chopped green
   pepper
1 tablespoon butter or margarine,
   melted
4 ears fresh corn
3 large eggs, lightly beaten
1 cup (4 ounces) shredded
   Cheddar cheese
1/4 cup all-purpose flour
1 tablespoon sugar
1/2 teaspoon salt

1/4 teaspoon ground red pepper
1/8 teaspoon ground nutmeg
2 cups half-and-half
2 tablespoons butter or
   margarine, melted
1 (2-ounce) jar diced pimiento,
   drained
1 small sweet red pepper, seeded
   and cut into 1/4-inch rings
1 small green pepper, seeded and
   cut into 1/4-inch rings

EQUIPMENT NEEDED:
- Grater
- Skillet
- 1½-quart shallow
  baking dish
- 13- x 9- x 2-inch pan

Sweet white corn
- White corn adds a hint of
sweetness to this rich summer
side dish.

Cook chopped green pepper in 1 tablespoon butter in a small skillet over medium-high heat, stirring constantly, until tender. Set aside.

Remove husks and silks from corn. Cut corn from cobs, scraping cobs to remove all milk. Measure 2 cups corn into a large bowl. Add cooked green pepper, eggs, and cheese; stir well.

Combine flour and next 4 ingredients, and add to corn mixture. Stir in half-and-half, 2 tablespoons butter, and pimiento. Pour mixture into a lightly greased 1½-quart shallow baking dish. Place dish in a 13- x 9- x 2-inch pan; pour hot water into pan to a depth of 1 inch.

Bake, uncovered, at 325° for 30 minutes. Arrange red and green pepper rings alternately over custard. Bake, uncovered, 40 additional minutes or until a knife inserted in center comes out clean. **Yield:** 8 servings.

ELEGANT
CORNISH HENS

GRILLED YELLOWFIN
TUNA STEAKS

Entrées

DELUXE POT ROAST

Beef Kabobs Supreme

Cleaning mushrooms

- Gently clean mushrooms with a mushroom brush or damp paper towel. Don't soak mushrooms in water; they'll absorb it and become spongy.

2 pounds beef tenderloin, cut into 1-inch cubes
¾ cup dry red wine
½ cup vegetable oil
⅓ cup soy sauce
¼ cup Worcestershire sauce
2 teaspoons dried rosemary, crushed
2 teaspoons coarsely ground pepper
1 teaspoon dried thyme
4 large cloves garlic, minced

12 boiling onions
2 large sweet red peppers, seeded and cut into 1½-inch pieces
2 large sweet yellow peppers, seeded and cut into 1½-inch pieces
2 medium zucchini, cut into 1-inch pieces
12 large mushrooms
Vegetable cooking spray
Hot cooked rice

Place cubed beef in a large shallow container. Combine wine and next 7 ingredients; stir well. Pour marinade mixture over meat. Cover and marinate in refrigerator 30 minutes.

Cook onions in a small amount of boiling water 3 minutes; drain. Cook pepper pieces in a small amount of boiling water 1 minute; drain.

Drain meat, reserving marinade. Place marinade in a small saucepan; bring to a boil. Remove from heat; set aside. Alternate meat, onions, pepper pieces, zucchini, and mushrooms on 12 (12-inch) metal skewers.

Coat grill with cooking spray. Grill kabobs, covered with grill lid, over medium coals (300° to 350°) 6 to 8 minutes on each side or to desired degree of doneness, basting often with reserved marinade. Serve kabobs over rice. **Yield:** 6 servings.

Classic Beef Stroganoff

1 pound (½-inch-thick) boneless sirloin steak
½ pound sliced fresh mushrooms
¼ cup chopped onion
1 clove garlic, crushed
3 tablespoons butter or margarine, melted
2 tablespoons all-purpose flour
3 tablespoons dry sherry
1 tablespoon lemon juice
¼ teaspoon pepper
1 (10½-ounce) can beef consommé
1 (8-ounce) carton sour cream
Hot cooked noodles
Garnish: fresh parsley sprigs

EQUIPMENT NEEDED:
• Large skillet
• Large saucepan

Partially freeze steak; slice steak diagonally across grain into 3- x ¼-inch strips, and set aside.

  Cook mushrooms, onion, and garlic in butter in a large skillet over medium-high heat, stirring constantly, until vegetables are tender. Add steak, and cook over medium-high heat until browned, stirring often. Add flour and next 4 ingredients, stirring well. Bring to a boil; reduce heat, and simmer 15 minutes, stirring occasionally. Stir in sour cream; cook until thoroughly heated (do not boil). Serve over noodles. Garnish, if desired. **Yield:** 4 servings.

Note: To make Parslied Noodles, just toss 3 cups hot cooked medium egg noodles with 2 tablespoons butter and 1 tablespoon chopped parsley.

Country-Fried Steak

EQUIPMENT NEEDED:
- Meat mallet or rolling pin
- Large heavy skillet

2 pounds boneless top round steak
1 cup all-purpose flour
2 teaspoons salt
1 teaspoon pepper
½ teaspoon garlic salt
½ teaspoon onion salt
½ cup milk
2 large eggs, lightly beaten
½ cup vegetable oil
¼ cup all-purpose flour
1¼ cups milk
½ cup half-and-half
¼ cup brewed coffee
1½ teaspoons Worcestershire sauce
¾ teaspoon salt
¼ teaspoon pepper
Garnishes: tomato wedges, fresh parsley sprigs

Trim excess fat from steak. Pound steak to ¼-inch thickness, using a meat mallet or rolling pin; cut into 6 or 8 serving-size pieces.

Combine 1 cup flour and next 4 ingredients; stir well. Dredge steak in flour mixture; lightly pound floured steak. Combine ½ cup milk and eggs in a bowl; stir well. Dip steak into milk mixture; dredge again in flour mixture.

Pour oil into a large heavy skillet. Fry steak in hot oil (375°) until browned, turning once. Remove steak from skillet, and drain on paper towels. Transfer steak to a serving platter. Set aside; keep warm.

Drain pan drippings, reserving ¼ cup drippings in skillet. Add ¼ cup flour to reserved drippings; stir until smooth. Cook over medium heat, stirring constantly, until bubbly. Combine 1¼ cups milk and next 3 ingredients; stir well. Gradually add to mixture in skillet; cook, stirring constantly, until thickened and bubbly. Add ¾ teaspoon salt and ¼ teaspoon pepper; stir well. Serve steak with gravy. Garnish, if desired. **Yield:** 6 to 8 servings.

Deluxe Pot Roast

1 (4- to 5-pound) boneless chuck
   roast
2 large cloves garlic, sliced
½ teaspoon salt
½ teaspoon pepper
¼ cup all-purpose flour
⅓ cup olive oil
1 medium onion, sliced
1 cup dry red wine
1 (8-ounce) can tomato sauce

1 tablespoon brown sugar
1 teaspoon dried oregano
1 teaspoon prepared horseradish
1 teaspoon prepared mustard
1 bay leaf
8 small red potatoes, peeled
6 carrots, scraped and quartered
4 stalks celery, cut into 2-inch
   pieces
Garnish: fresh oregano sprigs

EQUIPMENT NEEDED:
• Dutch oven or large
  deep skillet
• Slotted spoon

Flavoring the roast

• Insert thin garlic slices into
slits in roast. This allows the
garlic flavor to permeate
the meat.

Make small slits in top of roast. Insert a garlic slice into each slit. Rub roast with salt and pepper; dredge in flour. Brown roast on all sides in hot oil in a Dutch oven or skillet. Add sliced onion and wine to roast in Dutch oven.

  Combine tomato sauce and next 4 ingredients; stir well. Pour over roast; add bay leaf. Bring liquid in Dutch oven to a boil; cover, reduce heat, and simmer 1½ hours. Add potatoes, carrot, and celery; cover and simmer 1 hour or until roast and vegetables are tender.

  Transfer roast to a serving platter; spoon vegetables around roast, using a slotted spoon. Discard bay leaf. Spoon any remaining pan drippings over roast and vegetables. Garnish roast, if desired. **Yield:** 8 to 10 servings.

Enchiladas with Red Sauce

1 pound ground beef
1 large onion, chopped
1 tablespoon plus 2 teaspoons all-purpose flour
1 tablespoon chili powder
2 teaspoons garlic powder
1 teaspoon salt
½ teaspoon ground cumin
¼ teaspoon rubbed sage
1 (14.5-ounce) can stewed tomatoes, undrained

Red Sauce
12 (6-inch) corn tortillas
1 cup finely chopped onion
1 cup sliced ripe olives
2 cups (8 ounces) shredded colby-Monterey Jack cheese blend
Sour cream
Additional sliced ripe olives

EQUIPMENT NEEDED:
• Grater
• Large skillet
• 13- x 9- x 2-inch baking dish

Softening tortillas

• Wrap tortillas in foil, and then heat 12 to 15 minutes to soften them so they won't crack when rolled.

Brown ground beef and large chopped onion in a large skillet, stirring until meat crumbles. Drain and return mixture to skillet. Add flour and next 5 ingredients, stirring well. Add stewed tomatoes; stir well. Bring to a boil; cover, reduce heat, and simmer 10 to 15 minutes, stirring occasionally.

Pour 1½ cups Red Sauce into a 13- x 9- x 2-inch baking dish. Set aside.

Wrap tortillas in aluminum foil. Heat at 350° for 12 to 15 minutes or until softened. Combine 1 cup chopped onion and 1 cup sliced olives. Working with 1 tortilla at a time, keeping remaining tortillas covered and warm, sprinkle 2 heaping tablespoonfuls onion-olive mixture down center of tortilla. Top with ¼ cup meat mixture. Roll tortilla tightly, and place in prepared dish, seam side down. Repeat with remaining tortillas. Pour remaining 2½ cups Red Sauce over tortillas. Cover and bake at 350° for 15 minutes. Uncover and sprinkle with cheese. Bake, uncovered, 5 additional minutes. Top enchiladas with sour cream and additional olives. **Yield:** 6 servings.

Red Sauce

8 cloves garlic, crushed
½ cup butter or margarine, melted
½ cup all-purpose flour
2 (8-ounce) cans tomato sauce

2 cups canned diluted beef broth
2 tablespoons chili powder
2 teaspoons rubbed sage
2 teaspoons ground cumin

Cook crushed garlic in butter 1 to 2 minutes, stirring often. Gradually stir in flour. Cook, stirring constantly, 1 minute. Gradually add tomato sauce and broth; add seasonings. Cook over medium heat, stirring constantly, until smooth and thickened. **Yield:** 4 cups.

Grillades and Grits

EQUIPMENT NEEDED:
- Meat mallet or rolling pin
- Dutch oven or stockpot
- Large saucepan

Creole brunch
- Grillade (gree-YAHD) is a Creole specialty of seared round steak that's braised in a rich brown sauce with tomatoes. It's commonly served with grits as a brunch dish.

2 pounds round steak
All-purpose flour
¾ cup vegetable oil, divided
½ cup all-purpose flour
1½ cups chopped green pepper
1 cup chopped onion
1 cup chopped green onions
1 cup chopped celery
2 cloves garlic, minced
2 (16-ounce) cans whole tomatoes, undrained

1 cup dry red wine
¼ cup Worcestershire sauce
2 teaspoons dried thyme
1 teaspoon salt
½ teaspoon pepper
½ teaspoon hot sauce
2 bay leaves
¼ cup chopped fresh parsley
Buttered Chive Grits
Garnish: chive knots

Trim fat from steak. Pound steak to ¼-inch thickness, using a meat mallet or rolling pin; cut into ¾-inch-wide strips. Dredge strips in flour. Heat 2 tablespoons oil in a Dutch oven; cook half of meat until browned on both sides. Remove to a large plate. Add 2 tablespoons oil to Dutch oven; brown remaining meat. Remove to plate.

Add ½ cup flour and remaining ½ cup oil to Dutch oven. Cook over medium-low heat, stirring constantly, until roux is the color of chocolate (30 to 45 minutes). Add green pepper and next 4 ingredients; cook until vegetables are tender. Add tomatoes and next 7 ingredients; stir well. Add browned meat; cover, reduce heat, and simmer 1 hour, stirring often. Uncover and simmer 30 additional minutes. Remove and discard bay leaves; stir in parsley. Serve with Buttered Chive Grits. Garnish, if desired. **Yield:** 8 servings.

Buttered Chive Grits

8 cups water
1 teaspoon salt
2 cups quick-cooking grits, uncooked

1 clove garlic, minced
¼ cup butter or margarine
¼ cup chopped fresh chives

Bring water and salt to a boil in a large saucepan; stir in grits and garlic. Return to a boil; reduce heat, and cook 4 to 6 minutes, stirring occasionally. Stir in butter and chives. **Yield:** 6½ cups.

Tournedos Diables

1 (4-pound) beef tenderloin
Coarsely ground black pepper
Garlic salt
12 slices bacon
2 cups canned diluted beef broth
¼ cup cognac
¼ cup sherry
2 tablespoons Dijon mustard
1 tablespoon butter or margarine
1 tablespoon tomato paste

1 tablespoon Worcestershire
   sauce
1 tablespoon white vinegar
½ teaspoon garlic powder
¼ teaspoon ground red pepper
1 cup sliced fresh mushrooms
⅔ cup chopped green onions
2 shallots, chopped
Hot cooked rice
Garnish: fresh parsley sprigs

Trim fat from beef. Slice into 12 (1-inch-thick) slices. Rub both sides of each slice with coarsely ground pepper and garlic salt. Wrap 1 slice bacon around each slice beef; secure with wooden picks.

   Bring broth to a boil in a heavy saucepan; reduce heat, and simmer 3 minutes. Heat cognac and sherry in a small saucepan just until hot (do not boil); remove from heat, ignite with a long match, and pour over broth. When flame dies down, add mustard and next 6 ingredients. Cook over low heat 15 minutes. Stir in mushrooms, green onions, and shallots. Cover and simmer 5 minutes.

   Grill bacon-wrapped tenderloin slices, covered with grill lid, over medium coals (300° to 350°) 10 minutes on each side or to desired degree of doneness. Remove wooden picks. Arrange tenderloin slices over rice on a platter; spoon mushroom sauce over meat. Garnish, if desired. **Yield:** 12 servings.

EQUIPMENT NEEDED:
• Wooden picks
• Heavy saucepan
• Small saucepan
• Grill

Sizing up steak

• A tournedo is a small steak cut from the tenderloin. It's at least 1-inch thick and about 2½ inches in diameter.

• Wrap 1 slice of bacon around each tournedo before grilling to add flavor and to hold the shape of the meat.

Individual Beef Wellingtons

EQUIPMENT NEEDED:
- Shallow dish
- Nonstick skillet
- Rolling pin
- Pastry brush or your fingers
- Broiler pan with rack
- Saucepan

Four fine herbs
- Fines Herbes (FEEN-erb) is a French term for a foursome of herbs—parsley, chives, tarragon, and chervil. Find it bottled in most supermarket spice sections.

Preparing pastry

- Brush edges of pastry squares with egg. Stretch pastry over each fillet; pinch edges to seal.

6 (4- to 5-ounce) filets mignons
Salt and freshly ground pepper
¾ teaspoon fines herbes
½ cup chopped onion
½ cup chopped celery
½ cup chopped carrot
1½ tablespoons vegetable oil
1 cup dry red wine
Mushroom Filling (facing page)
1 to 2 tablespoons butter or margarine, melted

6 frozen puff pastry shells, thawed
2 large eggs, lightly beaten
1 frozen puff pastry shell, thawed (optional)
1½ cups canned diluted beef broth
2 tablespoons tomato paste
2 tablespoons cornstarch
¼ cup Madeira
Garnishes: fluted mushrooms, fresh parsley sprigs

Place fillets in a shallow dish. Sprinkle with salt, pepper, and fines herbes. Cook onion, celery, and carrot in hot oil over medium-high heat, stirring constantly, until tender; add wine, stirring well. Pour mixture over fillets; cover and marinate in refrigerator 2 to 8 hours.

Prepare Mushroom Filling; cover and chill thoroughly.

Drain fillets, reserving marinade. Sear fillets on both sides in 1 to 2 tablespoons butter in a nonstick skillet over medium-high heat.

Roll each of 6 thawed pastry shells to a 7-inch square on a lightly floured surface; spread each square with ⅓ cup chilled Mushroom Filling. Top each with a fillet.

Brush edges of pastry squares with beaten eggs. Stretch pastry over each fillet, and pinch edges to seal. Place Wellingtons, seam side down, on a rack in a broiler pan. Brush top of each pastry with beaten eggs. If desired, roll 1 pastry shell to ⅛-inch thickness, and cut into decorative shapes; arrange on top of Wellingtons. Brush with remaining beaten eggs. Bake, uncovered, at 400° for 25 minutes or until golden.

Combine reserved marinade, beef broth, and tomato paste in a medium saucepan. Cover and simmer 1 hour. Combine cornstarch and Madeira; stir into broth mixture. Cook over medium heat, stirring constantly, until thickened. Serve with Wellingtons. Garnish, if desired. **Yield:** 6 servings.

Mushroom Filling

1 pound fresh mushrooms, finely
    chopped
2 shallots, minced
¾ teaspoon fines herbes

2 tablespoons butter or
    margarine, melted
½ cup Madeira
Salt and pepper to taste

Cook first 3 ingredients in butter in a large skillet over medium heat, stirring constantly, until all liquid evaporates. Add Madeira; cook until liquid
evaporates. Stir in salt and pepper. **Yield:** 2 cups.

Veal Piccata

⅔ cup all-purpose flour
1 teaspoon salt
½ teaspoon ground white pepper
¼ teaspoon black pepper
½ cup butter or margarine
2 cloves garlic

12 thin veal cutlets (about 1½ pounds)
4 to 6 tablespoons lemon juice
2 tablespoons chopped fresh parsley
Garnish: lemon twists

Combine first 4 ingredients in a small bowl; stir well, and set aside.

Melt butter in a large skillet over medium heat; add garlic, and cook, stirring constantly, until tender. Remove and discard garlic from skillet.

Dredge veal in flour mixture. Add veal to skillet, and cook, stirring constantly, 2 minutes on each side or until lightly browned; drain on paper towels. Add lemon juice to skillet; cook, stirring constantly, to loosen particles on bottom of skillet. Return veal to skillet; sprinkle with parsley, and cook 1 minute or until thoroughly heated.

Transfer veal to a serving platter. Spoon lemon juice mixture over veal. Garnish, if desired. **Yield:** 4 to 6 servings.

Autumn-Stuffed Pork Chops

¾ cup toasted raisin bread
    breadcrumbs
¼ cup diced unpeeled apple
¼ cup diced unpeeled pear
1½ tablespoons minced onion
1 tablespoon diced celery
1 tablespoon butter or
    margarine, melted
½ teaspoon sugar
¼ teaspoon salt
Dash of pepper

Pinch of ground sage
4 (1¼-inch-thick) pork chops,
    trimmed and cut with
    pockets on the side
Salt and pepper
1 tablespoon butter or
    margarine, melted
2 tablespoons apple juice
1 tablespoon water
Glazed Apple Rings
Garnish: fresh sage leaves

Combine first 10 ingredients; stir well. Fill pockets of pork chops with mixture; secure with wooden picks. Sprinkle chops with salt and pepper.

Brown chops on both sides in 1 tablespoon butter in a large skillet. Add juice and water; cover, reduce heat, and simmer 55 minutes or until chops are tender. Arrange chops on serving platter; surround with Glazed Apple Rings. Garnish, if desired. **Yield:** 4 servings.

Glazed Apple Rings

2 large red cooking apples
    (about 1 pound)
2 tablespoons lemon juice

¾ cup water
¼ cup sugar
2 tablespoons light corn syrup

Core apples. Slice apples into ½-inch-thick rings; toss with lemon juice. Combine water, sugar, and syrup in a skillet; bring to a boil. Boil, stirring constantly, 2 minutes or until sugar dissolves. Layer apple rings in skillet. Add any remaining lemon juice; reduce heat, and simmer 8 minutes or until apple rings are tender, turning once. **Yield:** about 1 dozen.

EQUIPMENT NEEDED:
• Wooden picks
• Large skillet
• Apple corer or small knife

Making crumbs
• Crumble 1½ slices raisin bread to yield ¾ cup crumbs; then place crumbs on baking sheet. Bake at 350° for 5 minutes or until toasted.

Filling pockets

• Fill pockets of pork chops with stuffing mixture, and secure with wooden picks.

Pork St. Tammany

2 (6-ounce) packages long-grain-
    and-wild rice mix
½ cup boiling water
½ cup chopped dried apricots
½ cup chopped fresh mushrooms
½ cup chopped green pepper
3 green onions, finely chopped
2 tablespoons butter or
    margarine, melted
⅔ cup chopped pecans, toasted

¼ cup chopped fresh parsley
¼ teaspoon salt
¼ teaspoon garlic powder
¼ teaspoon ground red pepper
¼ teaspoon black pepper
4 (¾-pound) pork tenderloins
½ cup apricot preserves, melted
2 tablespoons honey
8 slices centercut bacon

Cook rice according to package directions; set aside.

Pour boiling water over apricots; let stand 20 minutes to soften. Drain and set apricots aside. Cook mushrooms, green pepper, and green onions in butter in a large skillet over medium-high heat, stirring constantly, until tender. Add cooked rice, apricots, pecans, and next 5 ingredients; stir well.

Cut a lengthwise slit through top of each tenderloin to, but not through, bottom. Spoon 1 cup of rice mixture into opening of 1 tenderloin; place cut side of second tenderloin over rice mixture. Bring sides of meat together, and tie tenderloins together with heavy string at 3-inch intervals. Place on a rack in a roasting pan lined with aluminum foil. Repeat procedure with remaining 2 tenderloins and 1 cup rice mixture. Set remaining rice mixture aside, and keep warm. Combine preserves and honey. Brush mixture lightly over tenderloins.

Cover and bake at 375° for 25 minutes. Uncover and remove string. Crisscross bacon slices over tops of tenderloins; secure at base of each with wooden picks. Brush again with preserves mixture. Bake, uncovered, 35 to 40 additional minutes or until meat thermometer registers 160°, basting often with preserves mixture. Remove from oven, and let stand 5 minutes. Slice and serve with reserved rice mixture. **Yield:** 10 to 12 servings.

Herb Garden Chicken

⅓ cup chopped onion
⅓ cup scraped, diced carrot
⅓ cup diced celery
1 tablespoon chopped parsley
3 tablespoons dry white wine
1 (3½-pound) broiler-fryer
2 cloves garlic, halved
⅓ cup butter or margarine, melted

⅓ cup dry white wine
2 teaspoons chopped fresh basil
2 teaspoons chopped fresh oregano
2 teaspoons chopped fresh thyme
½ teaspoon salt
¼ teaspoon ground white pepper
Garnishes: fresh basil, oregano, and thyme sprigs

Combine first 5 ingredients; toss gently. Set aside. Remove giblets and neck from chicken; reserve for another use. Rinse chicken with cold water; pat dry with paper towels. Rub skin of chicken with cut side of each garlic clove half. Lightly stuff chicken with garlic clove halves and reserved vegetable mixture. Close cavity with skewers; tie ends of legs together with string or cord. Lift wingtips up and over back of chicken, tucking wingtips under chicken. Place chicken, breast side up, on a rack in a shallow roasting pan.

Combine melted butter and next 6 ingredients in a small bowl; stir well. Brush chicken generously with butter mixture.

Bake, uncovered, at 375° for 1½ hours or until chicken is done, basting occasionally with any remaining butter mixture. Place chicken on a serving platter. Garnish, if desired. **Yield:** 4 servings.

Golden Fruited Chicken

6 (4-ounce) chicken breast
    halves, skinned
1 teaspoon ground ginger
¼ teaspoon salt
⅛ teaspoon pepper
⅛ teaspoon dried rosemary,
    crushed
2 cups orange marmalade
¼ cup apple juice

¼ cup orange juice
8 ounces dried apricots (about
    1¼ cups)
8 ounces golden raisins (about
    1½ cups)
⅓ cup firmly packed brown
    sugar
Garnishes: fresh rosemary sprigs,
    orange rind strips

EQUIPMENT NEEDED:
• Roasting pan
• Saucepan
• Basting bulb, brush,
  or spoon

Place chicken breast halves in a lightly greased shallow roasting pan.
Combine ginger and next 3 ingredients; sprinkle over chicken.

  Place marmalade in a small saucepan. Cook over low heat just until softened.
Stir in apple juice and orange juice. Pour marmalade mixture over chicken,
coating well. Bake, uncovered, at 375° for 20 minutes.

  Remove from oven; add apricots and raisins to liquid in pan. Sprinkle entire
mixture with brown sugar. Bake 30 to 40 additional minutes or until golden,
basting often with pan juices.

  Arrange chicken and fruit on a serving platter. Pour some of pan juices over
chicken. Garnish, if desired. Serve immediately. **Yield:** 6 servings.

Chicken Bundles

6 whole chicken breasts, skinned and boned
½ cup molasses
¼ cup olive oil
¼ cup lemon juice
¼ cup soy sauce
2 tablespoons Worcestershire sauce
½ teaspoon ground ginger
¼ teaspoon garlic powder
¼ cup butter or margarine
¾ pound mushrooms, sliced
½ teaspoon salt
¼ teaspoon pepper
10 green onions, sliced
12 slices bacon
Vegetable cooking spray
Hot cooked rice (optional)

Place each chicken breast between two sheets of heavy-duty plastic wrap; flatten to ¼-inch thickness, using a meat mallet or rolling pin. Place chicken in a large shallow baking dish. Combine molasses and next 6 ingredients; stir well. Pour over chicken; cover and marinate in refrigerator 8 hours, turning chicken occasionally.

Melt butter in a large skillet; add mushrooms and next 3 ingredients. Cook over medium-high heat until liquid evaporates and vegetables are tender, stirring often.

Remove chicken from baking dish, reserving marinade. Pour marinade into a small saucepan; bring to a boil. Remove from heat, and set aside. For each chicken bundle, place 2 slices bacon in a crisscross pattern on a flat surface. Place 1 chicken breast in center of bacon. Top with 3 tablespoons mushroom mixture. Fold sides and ends of chicken over mushroom mixture to make a square-shaped pouch. Pull bacon around chicken, and tie ends of bacon together; secure with wooden picks.

Coat grill with cooking spray. Place chicken bundles on grill, tied side up; grill, covered with grill lid, over low coals 30 to 45 minutes or until done, turning and basting with reserved marinade every 15 minutes. Remove wooden picks. Serve over hot cooked rice, if desired. **Yield:** 6 servings.

Chicken Breasts Lombardy

2 cups sliced fresh mushrooms
2 tablespoons butter or
   margarine, melted
12 skinned and boned chicken
   breast halves
½ cup all-purpose flour
⅓ cup butter or margarine,
   melted and divided

¾ cup Marsala
½ cup chicken broth
½ teaspoon salt
⅛ teaspoon pepper
½ cup (2 ounces) shredded
   mozzarella cheese
½ cup grated Parmesan cheese
¼ cup chopped green onions

Cook mushrooms in 2 tablespoons butter in a large skillet, stirring constantly, just until tender. Remove from heat; set aside.

Cut each chicken breast half in half lengthwise. Place each piece of chicken between two sheets of wax paper; flatten to ⅛-inch thickness, using a meat mallet or rolling pin.

Dredge chicken pieces in flour. Place 5 or 6 pieces of chicken in 1 to 2 tablespoons butter in a large skillet; cook over medium heat 3 to 4 minutes on each side or until golden. Place chicken in a lightly greased 13- x 9- x 2-inch baking dish or other large casserole, overlapping edges. Repeat procedure with remaining chicken and butter. Reserve pan drippings in skillet. Sprinkle reserved mushrooms over chicken.

Add wine and broth to skillet. Bring to a boil; reduce heat, and simmer, uncovered, 10 minutes, stirring occasionally. Stir in salt and pepper. Pour sauce over chicken. Combine cheeses and green onions; sprinkle over chicken.

Bake, uncovered, at 450° for 12 to 14 minutes. Broil 5½ inches from heat (with electric oven door partially opened) 1 to 2 minutes or until browned.
Yield: 6 to 8 servings.

Creamy Chicken Tetrazzini

EQUIPMENT NEEDED:
- Grater
- Dutch oven or stockpot
- 13- x 9- x 2-inch baking dish

1 (3- to 4-pound) broiler-fryer
1 teaspoon salt
1 teaspoon pepper
1 (8-ounce) package spaghetti
1 cup sliced fresh mushrooms
1 large green pepper, seeded and chopped
1 small onion, chopped
¼ cup butter or margarine, melted
¼ cup all-purpose flour
½ teaspoon salt
½ teaspoon garlic powder
½ teaspoon poultry seasoning

½ teaspoon pepper
1 cup half-and-half
2 cups (8 ounces) shredded sharp Cheddar cheese, divided
1 (10¾-ounce) can cream of mushroom soup, undiluted
¾ cup grated Parmesan cheese, divided
¼ cup sherry
1 (4-ounce) jar sliced pimiento, drained
1 teaspoon paprika
¾ cup sliced almonds, toasted

Place broiler-fryer in a Dutch oven; add water to cover. Add 1 teaspoon salt and 1 teaspoon pepper, and bring to a boil. Cover, reduce heat, and simmer 1 hour or until chicken is tender. Remove chicken from broth, reserving broth. Let chicken cool to touch. Bone and shred chicken.

Add enough water to reserved broth to measure 3 quarts. Bring to a boil. Cook spaghetti in broth according to package directions. Drain.

Cook mushrooms, green pepper, and onion in butter in Dutch oven over medium heat, stirring constantly, until tender. Add flour and next 4 ingredients; stir until smooth. Cook, stirring constantly, 1 minute. Gradually stir in half-and-half, and cook until thickened, stirring gently. Add ¾ cup Cheddar cheese, stirring until cheese melts. Add shredded chicken, mushroom soup, ½ cup Parmesan cheese, sherry, and pimiento; stir well.

Combine chicken mixture and cooked spaghetti, tossing until combined. Spread mixture into a greased 13- x 9- 2-inch baking dish.

Bake, uncovered, at 350° for 20 to 25 minutes or until thoroughly heated. Combine remaining ¼ cup Parmesan cheese and paprika; stir well. Sprinkle remaining 1¼ cups Cheddar cheese in diagonal rows across top of casserole. Repeat procedure with sliced almonds and Parmesan-paprika mixture. Bake 5 additional minutes or until Cheddar cheese melts. **Yield:** 6 to 8 servings.

Soy-Lime Grilled Chicken Thighs

EQUIPMENT NEEDED:
- 11- x 7- x 1½-inch baking dish
- Saucepan
- Grill

Multipurpose marinade
- This Caribbean-style marinade also tastes great on pork tenderloin or other cuts of chicken.

8 large chicken thighs, skinned
½ cup soy sauce
¼ cup chopped green onions
¼ cup lime juice
2 tablespoons dark brown sugar
1 tablespoon honey

1 teaspoon dried crushed red pepper
1 large clove garlic, crushed
Garnishes: lime wedges, fresh parsley sprigs

Place chicken thighs in an 11- x 7- x 1½-inch baking dish. Combine soy sauce and next 6 ingredients; stir well. Pour over chicken. Cover and marinate in refrigerator 8 hours, turning occasionally.

Drain chicken thighs, reserving marinade. Place marinade in a small saucepan; bring to a boil. Grill chicken thighs, covered with grill lid, over medium coals (300° to 350°) 8 minutes on each side or until done, basting often with marinade. Garnish, if desired. **Yield:** 4 servings.

Smothered Quail with Vegetables

12 quail, dressed
Salt and pepper
⅔ cup all-purpose flour
Vegetable oil
2½ cups chicken broth
¼ cup molasses
2 tablespoons Worcestershire
　　sauce
1 tablespoon lemon juice
1 teaspoon poultry seasoning

1 clove garlic, crushed
½ pound fresh mushrooms,
　　halved
4 stalks celery, cut into 2-inch
　　pieces
3 large carrots, scraped and
　　sliced
½ cup dry white wine
4 green onions, chopped

Sprinkle quail with salt and pepper; dredge in flour. Pour oil to depth of
½ inch in a large heavy skillet. Brown quail in hot oil. Remove quail;
discard oil. Return quail to skillet. Combine chicken broth and next 5
ingredients; add to skillet. Bring to a boil; cover, reduce heat, and simmer
30 minutes. Add mushrooms and next 3 ingredients. Cover mixture, and
simmer 30 minutes. Add green onions just before serving. **Yield:** 6 servings.

EQUIPMENT NEEDED:
- Large heavy skillet
- Tongs or long-handled fork

Browning quail

- Brown the seasoned quail in
hot oil in a large heavy skillet.

Double-Crust Chicken Pot Pie

6 skinned and boned chicken breast halves, cut into 1-inch pieces
1 medium onion, chopped
2 tablespoons butter or margarine, melted
1 cup sliced fresh mushrooms
1 cup chicken broth
3/4 cup scraped, chopped carrot
3/4 cup frozen English peas
3/4 cup peeled, chopped potato
1/4 cup dry white wine
1/2 teaspoon dried parsley flakes
1/4 teaspoon ground white pepper
1 stalk celery, chopped
1 bay leaf
2 tablespoons cornstarch
2 tablespoons water
1 (10¾-ounce) can cream of mushroom soup, undiluted
1/2 cup sour cream
3/4 cup (3 ounces) shredded Cheddar cheese

Celery Seed Pastry
1 egg yolk, lightly beaten
1 tablespoon half-and-half or milk

EQUIPMENT NEEDED:
• Grater
• Dutch oven or stockpot
• Rolling pin
• Deep 2-quart casserole
• Pastry brush
• Pastry blender or two knives

What's an egg wash?

• Brush egg yolk and cream over pastry before baking. This "egg wash" helps the pastry become a rich, glossy golden crust.

Cook chicken and onion in butter in a Dutch oven over medium-high heat, stirring constantly, 5 minutes. Stir in mushrooms and next 9 ingredients. Bring mixture to a boil; cover, reduce heat, and simmer 15 minutes or until vegetables are tender. Remove and discard bay leaf.

Combine cornstarch and water, stirring until blended; add to chicken mixture. Cook over medium heat, stirring constantly, until mixture comes to a boil. Remove from heat; stir in soup, sour cream, and cheese.

Roll half of Celery Seed Pastry to ⅛-inch thickness on a floured surface. Fit pastry into an ungreased deep 2-quart casserole. Spoon chicken mixture into prepared pastry. Roll remaining pastry to ⅛-inch thickness, and place over chicken mixture; trim, seal, and flute edges. Reroll pastry trimmings, and make chicken-shaped cutouts. Dampen cutouts with water, and arrange on top of pastry. Cut slits in pastry.

Combine egg yolk and half-and-half; brush egg wash mixture over pastry. Bake at 400° for 30 minutes or until golden. Shield pastry with aluminum foil to prevent excessive browning, if necessary. **Yield:** 6 servings.

Celery Seed Pastry

3 cups all-purpose flour
2 teaspoons celery seeds
1 teaspoon salt
1 cup shortening
4 to 6 tablespoons cold water

Combine first 3 ingredients; cut in shortening with pastry blender until mixture is crumbly. Sprinkle cold water (1 tablespoon at a time) evenly over surface; stir with a fork until dry ingredients are moistened. Shape dough into a ball; chill. **Yield:** pastry for one double-crust pie.

Roast Turkey and Cornbread Stuffing

1 (12- to 14-pound) turkey
Cornbread Stuffing
½ cup butter or margarine, melted
Salt and pepper
Garnishes: curly endive, red grape clusters, orange wedges

Remove giblets and neck from turkey; reserve for another use. Rinse turkey thoroughly inside and out with cold water; pat dry. Lightly pack Cornbread Stuffing into body cavities of turkey. Tuck legs under flap of skin around tail; or close cavity with skewers, and truss. Tie ends of legs together with cord. Lift wingtips up and over back, and tuck under turkey.

Place turkey on a rack in a roasting pan, breast side up; brush entire surface of bird with butter. Sprinkle with salt and pepper. Insert meat thermometer into meaty part of thigh, making sure it does not touch bone.

Bake turkey at 325° for 3 hours, basting often with butter. If turkey starts to brown too much, cover with aluminum foil. Cut cord holding drumsticks to tail to ensure that thighs are cooked internally. Bake 1 to 2 additional hours or until meat thermometer registers 180°. Turkey is done when drumsticks are easy to move up and down. Let turkey stand 15 minutes before carving. Garnish, if desired. **Yield:** 20 servings.

Cornbread Stuffing

6 cups crumbled cornbread
5 slices day-old bread, crumbled
1 pound ground pork sausage, cooked and drained
1½ cups finely chopped cooked ham
¾ cup hazelnuts, toasted and chopped
¾ cup chopped fresh parsley
1½ teaspoons freshly ground pepper
1 teaspoon poultry seasoning
1 teaspoon rubbed sage
4 stalks celery, chopped
2 medium onions, chopped
¼ cup butter or margarine, melted
2 cups chicken or turkey broth
1 large egg, lightly beaten

Combine first 9 ingredients in a large bowl; toss well. Cook celery and onion in butter in a large skillet over medium-high heat, stirring constantly, until tender. Add to cornbread mixture, stirring gently. Add broth and egg to cornbread mixture; stir well. **Yield:** 13 cups.

Note: Stuffing may be spooned into a greased 13- x 9- x 2-inch baking pan. Bake, uncovered, at 350° for 45 minutes to 1 hour or until browned.

You Will Need

FOR THE FRUIT SALAD

1 large watermelon (about 15 pounds)
2 cantaloupe melons
2 honeydew melons
½ cup sugar
½ cup fresh lime juice
¼ cup fresh lemon juice
2 tablespoons orange-flavored liqueur (optional)
2 teaspoons grated lime peel
3 cups sliced fresh strawberries, washed, hulled and halved
2 cups black or red seedless grapes, washed and halved

SPECIAL AIDS

water-soluble marker
melon baller
vegetable peeler

SERVES 18

Kitchen Tips

It's important to purchase watermelons that are fully ripe, since they don't continue to ripen once they've been picked. A ripe melon feels heavy for its size and has a sweet, fresh fragrance.

Step by Step

CARVING THE BASKET

1. Lay a dampened dish towel on a counter or table and place melon on top to prevent it from rolling.

2. With a water-soluble marker, draw outline of basket onto melon, making sure the handle is at least 1¼ inches wide. ▼

3. Using a large sharp knife, carefully cut melon along marker line. ▼

4. Remove excess rind and set aside. With a melon baller, scoop out all the watermelon flesh and place in a large glass or ceramic bowl; set aside.

5. With a vegetable peeler, even out scalloped edges of watermelon. Cover watermelon basket with clear plastic wrap and set aside. ▼

MAKING THE FRUIT SALAD

1. With a melon baller, scoop out flesh from cantaloupes and honeydews.

2. In a large bowl, combine sugar, lime juice, lemon juice, orange liqueur and lime peel. Stir well.

3. Add all melon balls, strawberries and grapes; toss to combine. Allow fruit to chill in refrigerator for 30 minutes.

4. Just before serving, transfer fruit salad to watermelon basket.

Attention to Detail

Follow any one of these decorative patterns to carve the edge of your watermelon basket.

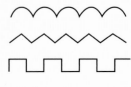

10124 20038 1001 ©MCMXCVIII International Masters Publishers AB. Creative Cook's Kitchen™ IMP AB, produced under license by IMP Inc. Packet 0. To collect more recipes, please contact: Creative Cook's Kitchen, 444 Liberty Avenue, Pittsburgh, PA 15222 (800) 335-6972. www.creativecookskitchen.com

Fruit Salad Basket

Make Ahead
Make the fruit salad portion up to 1 day ahead. Cover with plastic wrap and refrigerate.

Easy Substitute
Kiwifruit, peeled and cut into quarters, makes a delicious substitute for the berries in this recipe.

Simple Elegance
Offer this fruit salad as a tasty dessert. Serve it, without the melon basket, in small crystal bowls. Top with a small mound of lemon sorbet and garnish with a sprig of mint.

**PREPARATION TIME
45 minutes**

GOOD IDEA Use the fruit salad to create colorful ice cubes. Serve them with fruit punch or lemonade for a cool treat.

Variations

For a Children's Party
To make a whale-shaped watermelon bowl, first sketch the body design on the melon; use a sharp knife to cut it out. Use celery stalks for the water spout.

Baby Shower Idea
For a baby shower, make this clever baby carriage basket. Shape excess rind into a handle and attach grapefruit halves for wheels.

Elegant Cornish Hens

EQUIPMENT NEEDED:
- Saucepan
- Wooden picks
- Heavy string
- Roasting pan with rack
- Basting brush

Apple garnish

- Follow directions in note at bottom of page to make these decorative apples.

½ cup sliced green onions
¼ cup minced celery
2 tablespoons butter or margarine, melted
1 tablespoon lemon juice
1 (6-ounce) package long-grain-and-wild rice mix
1½ cups chicken broth
½ cup apple juice
½ cup unpeeled, chopped Red Delicious apple

¼ cup chopped pecans, toasted
2 tablespoons minced parsley
6 (1½-pound) Cornish hens
Salt and pepper
¼ cup apple jelly
2 tablespoons butter or margarine
2 tablespoons apple brandy
Garnishes: Red Delicious and Granny Smith apple slices, lemon juice, fresh parsley

Cook onions and celery in 2 tablespoons melted butter and 1 tablespoon lemon juice in a saucepan over medium-high heat, stirring constantly, until vegetables are tender. Add rice mix, broth, and apple juice; stir. Bring to a boil; cover, reduce heat, and simmer 25 minutes or until liquid is absorbed. Remove from heat. Stir in chopped apple, pecans, and minced parsley.

Remove giblets from hens; reserve for another use. Rinse hens with cold water; pat dry. Sprinkle cavities of hens with salt and pepper. Lift wingtips up and over back of hens, tucking wingtips under hens. Stuff hens lightly with rice mixture; close cavities. Secure with wooden picks, and tie legs together with string.

Combine apple jelly, 2 tablespoons butter, and brandy in a small saucepan; cook over low heat until jelly and butter melt, stirring often.

Place hens, breast side up, on a greased rack in a shallow roasting pan. Brush hens with jelly mixture. Bake at 350° for 1½ hours or until juices run clear when thigh is pierced with a fork, basting often with any remaining jelly mixture. Garnish hens, if desired. **Yield:** 6 servings.

Note: To make decorative apple garnishes, quarter apples lengthwise; discard cores. Cut each apple quarter into 4 wedge-shaped slices; separate apple slices to form a winged design. Brush apples with lemon juice.

Crabmeat Imperial

¼ cup chopped green pepper
¼ cup chopped celery
1 (2-ounce) jar diced pimiento, drained
2 tablespoons butter or margarine, melted
1 teaspoon Old Bay seasoning
1 teaspoon butter-flavored salt
2 teaspoons chopped parsley
½ teaspoon prepared mustard
Dash of hot sauce
Dash of ground red pepper
1 large egg, lightly beaten
3 tablespoons mayonnaise
1 pound fresh lump crabmeat, drained
Mayonnaise
Garnishes: pimiento strips and celery leaves

Cook first 3 ingredients in butter over medium-high heat, stirring constantly, until tender. Add Old Bay seasoning and next 5 ingredients; stir.

Combine egg and 3 tablespoons mayonnaise; stir in vegetable mixture. Gently stir in crabmeat. Spoon mixture into four lightly greased baking shells. Place shells on a baking sheet. Bake at 375° for 15 minutes. Broil 5½ inches from heat (with electric oven door partially opened) 2 to 3 minutes or until golden. Top each serving with a dollop of mayonnaise. Garnish, if desired. **Yield:** 4 servings.

EQUIPMENT NEEDED:
• Skillet
• Four baking shells
• Baking sheet

Garnishing crab

• Top each serving of broiled crabmeat with mayonnaise and colorful garnishes.

Crawfish Étouffée

EQUIPMENT NEEDED:
- Large saucepan
- Large cast-iron skillet or Dutch oven
- Wire whisk

What's étouffée?
- Étouffée is a French term that means "smothered." This étouffée uses crawfish tail meat and is smothered in a dark rich Creole sauce.

4½ pounds whole, cooked fresh or frozen crawfish, thawed
½ teaspoon hot sauce
½ cup vegetable oil
½ cup all-purpose flour
½ cup chopped celery
½ cup chopped green onions
1 tablespoon tomato paste
3 cloves garlic, minced
2 large green peppers, seeded and chopped
1 large onion, chopped
½ teaspoon salt
¼ teaspoon ground red pepper
¼ teaspoon Creole seasoning
Hot cooked rice
Garnish: chopped fresh parsley

Peel crawfish, removing tail meat (about 2½ cups). Reserve 1 tablespoon of yellow fat from tail meat; sprinkle tails with hot sauce. Set aside. Place half of crawfish shells in a large saucepan; add water to cover. Bring to a boil. Cover, reduce heat, and simmer 10 minutes. Remove from heat, and set crawfish stock aside.

Combine oil and flour in a large cast-iron skillet or Dutch oven. Cook over medium heat, stirring constantly with a wire whisk, 20 to 30 minutes or until roux is the color of chocolate. Add celery and next 5 ingredients. Cook, stirring constantly, 3 minutes.

Strain crawfish stock, reserving ½ cup stock. Discard crawfish shells. Add crawfish tails, 1 tablespoon reserved fat, ½ cup stock, salt, red pepper, and Creole seasoning to skillet. Cook, uncovered, over low heat 15 minutes or to desired degree of thickness. Serve with rice. Garnish, if desired. **Yield:** 4 to 6 servings.

Lobster Newburg

1½ (17¼-ounce) packages frozen puff pastry, thawed
2 quarts water
4 (8-ounce) frozen lobster tails, thawed
1 cup sliced fresh mushrooms
¼ cup chopped green onions
¼ cup minced green pepper
2 tablespoons butter, melted
1 (2-ounce) jar diced pimiento

¼ cup dry sherry
2 tablespoons butter
1 tablespoon all-purpose flour
1 cup whipping cream
½ teaspoon dry mustard
¼ teaspoon ground nutmeg
⅛ teaspoon ground red pepper
Dash of salt and paprika
Garnish: steamed artichoke leaves

EQUIPMENT NEEDED:
• Baking sheets
• Wire cooling racks
• Dutch oven or large stockpot
• Tongs
• Large skillet
• Heavy saucepan

Artichoke garnish
• If you boil artichokes for a side dish to accompany the lobster, you'll automatically have your garnish ready.

Cut puff pastry into 12 (5-inch) seashell shapes. Place pastry shells on ungreased baking sheets. Using a sharp knife, score top of each shell several times by cutting to, but not through, bottom of pastry to form the shell design. Bake at 350° for 20 minutes or until puffed. Let cool on wire racks.

Bring 2 quarts water to a boil in a Dutch oven; add lobster tails. Return to a boil; cook 5 minutes. Remove lobster tails with tongs; rinse with cold water. Drain. Split tails lengthwise. Remove and coarsely chop meat.

Cook mushrooms, green onions, and green pepper in 2 tablespoons melted butter in a large skillet over medium-high heat, stirring constantly, 2 minutes or until vegetables are tender. Drain pimiento. Stir pimiento and sherry into vegetable mixture, and cook 1 minute. Remove from heat; set aside.

Melt 2 tablespoons butter in a heavy saucepan over low heat; add flour, stirring until smooth. Cook, stirring constantly, 1 minute. Gradually add whipping cream; cook over medium heat, stirring constantly, until mixture is slightly thickened and bubbly. Stir in vegetable mixture. Combine mustard, nutmeg, red pepper, salt, and paprika; add to sauce mixture, stirring well. Stir lobster meat into sauce mixture; cook just until heated. Remove from heat.

Place half of pastry shells, scored side down, on individual serving plates. Spoon lobster mixture evenly over shells. Top with remaining pastry shells, scored side up. Garnish, if desired. **Yield:** 6 servings.

EQUIPMENT NEEDED:
• 13- x 9- x 2-inch baking dish

Preparing shrimp

• Layer shrimp, lemon slices, and onion slices in baking dish. Pour butter mixture over layers.

Buy a baguette
• Be sure to serve the flavorful pan juices along with this spicy shrimp. Buy a crusty French baguette to sop up the juices.

Southern–Style Barbecued Shrimp

1 cup butter or margarine, melted	2 to 3 teaspoons hot sauce
¾ cup lemon juice	⅛ teaspoon ground red pepper
¾ cup Worcestershire sauce	3 cloves garlic, minced
1 tablespoon salt	2½ pounds unpeeled large or jumbo fresh shrimp
1 tablespoon coarsely ground black pepper	2 lemons, thinly sliced
1 tablespoon fresh rosemary or 1 teaspoon dried rosemary	1 medium onion, thinly sliced
	Garnish: fresh rosemary sprigs

Combine first 9 ingredients in a small bowl; stir well, and set aside.

Rinse shrimp; drain. Layer shrimp, lemon slices, and onion slices in a 13- x 9- x 2-inch baking dish. Pour reserved butter mixture over shrimp.

Bake, uncovered, at 400° for 20 to 25 minutes or until shrimp turn pink and shells start to pull away, basting occasionally with pan juices. Garnish, if desired. **Yield:** 6 servings.

166   *Entrées*

Walnut-Fried Shrimp

16 unpeeled jumbo fresh shrimp
2 cups all-purpose flour
¼ teaspoon pepper
⅛ teaspoon salt
2 large eggs, lightly beaten
1 cup milk

2 cups ground walnuts
Vegetable oil
Cocktail sauce
Tartar sauce
Garnishes: lemon wedges, fresh
    parsley sprigs

EQUIPMENT NEEDED:

- Baking sheet
- Deep-fat fryer

Peel and devein shrimp, leaving tails intact; rinse well, and set aside.

  Combine flour, pepper, and salt; stir well. Combine eggs and milk; stir well. Dip shrimp in egg mixture; dredge in flour mixture. Dip shrimp in egg mixture again, and dredge in ground walnuts. Place coated shrimp on a wax paper-lined baking sheet; cover and freeze 2 hours.

  Fry shrimp, a few at a time, in deep hot oil (350°) 3 minutes or until golden. Drain on paper towels.

  Arrange shrimp on a serving platter. Serve with cocktail sauce and tartar sauce. Garnish, if desired. **Yield:** 4 servings.

Freeze before frying

- Place coated shrimp on lined baking sheet; cover and freeze to keep the coating intact while frying.

Fry a few

- Fry shrimp in deep hot oil a few at a time to maintain a consistent oil temperature.

Almond-Coated Trout

6 large trout fillets (about 3 pounds)
½ cup milk
¼ cup butter or margarine, melted
½ teaspoon almond extract
⅓ cup all-purpose flour
⅓ cup yellow cornmeal
½ teaspoon salt

½ teaspoon pepper
1¼ cups slivered almonds, minced
¾ cup coarsely crushed corn flakes cereal
½ cup almond, peanut, or vegetable oil
Garnish: fresh parsley sprigs

Rinse trout with cold water; pat dry, and set aside.

Combine milk, butter, and almond extract; stir well, and set aside. Combine flour and next 3 ingredients; stir well, and set aside. Combine almonds and cereal; toss gently. Dip trout in milk mixture; dredge in flour mixture. Dip again in milk mixture; coat with almond-cereal mixture.

Heat oil in a large heavy skillet. Fry trout, a few at a time, in hot oil 3 to 4 minutes on each side or until golden. Drain on paper towels. Garnish, if desired. **Yield:** 6 servings.

Variation: To bake Almond-Coated Trout, omit ½ cup oil. Place coated trout fillets on a rack in a broiler pan. Bake at 500° for 4 minutes on each side or until fish flakes easily when tested with a fork.

Grilled Yellowfin Tuna Steaks

4 yellowfin tuna steaks (about 2 pounds)

⅓ cup olive oil

3 tablespoons lemon juice

½ teaspoon coarsely ground pepper

2 cloves garlic, crushed

1 small sweet red pepper, cut in half lengthwise and seeded

1 small purple onion, cut in half crosswise

½ cup butter, softened

¼ teaspoon coarsely ground pepper

1 clove garlic, crushed

⅓ cup finely chopped tomato

1 tablespoon chopped fresh cilantro

1 tablespoon lemon juice

1 tablespoon lime juice

2 teaspoons sugar

1 teaspoon olive oil

Dash of salt

Garnish: fresh cilantro sprigs

EQUIPMENT NEEDED:
- 13- x 9- x 2-inch baking dish
- Grill
- Electric mixer or wooden spoon
- Saucepan

Place tuna steaks in a 13- x 9- x 2-inch baking dish. Combine ⅓ cup oil and next 3 ingredients in a small bowl; stir well. Pour mixture over tuna. Cover and marinate in refrigerator 2 hours, turning once.

Grill red pepper and onion pieces, covered with grill lid, over medium coals (300° to 350°) 3 to 4 minutes or just until charred but still crisp, turning once. Mince onion and red pepper; press between paper towels to remove excess moisture. Set aside.

Combine softened butter, ¼ teaspoon pepper, and 1 clove crushed garlic in a medium bowl; beat at medium speed of an electric mixer until smooth. Stir in 2 tablespoons minced red pepper and 1 tablespoon minced onion. Chill butter mixture 15 minutes or until firm enough to shape. Shape mixture into a log. Wrap in wax paper, and chill until firm.

Combine remaining minced red pepper, onion, tomato, and next 6 ingredients in a small bowl. Stir well, and chill.

Remove tuna steaks from marinade, reserving marinade. Place marinade in a small saucepan; bring to a boil. Grill steaks over medium coals (300° to 350°) 6 minutes on each side or until fish flakes easily when tested with a fork, basting often with reserved marinade. Transfer steaks to a serving plate. Cut butter into 8 pieces; place 2 pats of butter over each tuna steak. Serve with minced red pepper-onion relish. Garnish, if desired. **Yield:** 4 servings.

SPANISH RICE CUPS

SPINACH-STUFFED LASAGNA RUFFLES

Pasta, Rice & Grains

PASTA PRIMAVERA

Specialty Lasagna

6 lasagna noodles, uncooked
1½ pounds ground beef
¾ cup chopped onion
3 large cloves garlic, minced
¼ cup red wine vinegar
2 teaspoons Italian seasoning
½ teaspoon dried oregano
¼ teaspoon salt
¼ teaspoon pepper
2 (8-ounce) cans tomato sauce
1 (6-ounce) can tomato paste
1 (4-ounce) can sliced
    mushrooms, drained

1 (8-ounce) package cream
    cheese, softened
¾ cup ricotta cheese
½ cup sour cream
1 large egg, lightly beaten
1¼ cups (5 ounces) shredded
    mozzarella cheese
½ cup grated Parmesan cheese
1 (6-ounce) package mozzarella
    cheese slices, cut into
    ½-inch-wide strips

Cook lasagna noodles according to package directions. Drain.

    Cook beef, onion, and garlic in a large skillet over medium-high heat until meat is browned and onion is tender, stirring until meat crumbles. Drain. Stir in vinegar and next 7 ingredients. Simmer 3 to 4 minutes. Remove from heat.

    Beat cream cheese at medium speed of an electric mixer until smooth. Stir in ricotta cheese, sour cream, and egg.

    Layer half each of noodles, cream cheese mixture, and meat mixture in a lightly greased 13- x 9- x 2-inch baking dish. Sprinkle with shredded mozzarella cheese. Repeat layers. Sprinkle with Parmesan cheese.

    Cover and bake at 350° for 40 minutes. Uncover and arrange mozzarella strips in a lattice design over lasagna. Bake, uncovered, 5 additional minutes. Let stand 5 minutes. **Yield:** 6 to 8 servings.

EQUIPMENT NEEDED:
- Grater
- Dutch oven or large stockpot
- Large skillet
- Electric mixer or wooden spoon
- 13- x 9- x 2-inch baking dish

Mozzarella topping

- Arrange mozzarella strips in a lattice design over lasagna, and bake again until cheese melts.

Spinach-Stuffed Lasagna Ruffles

1 (8-ounce) package lasagna
   noodles, uncooked
1 (8-ounce) package cream
   cheese, softened
2 (10-ounce) packages frozen
   chopped spinach, thawed and
   drained
1 (15-ounce) carton ricotta
   cheese

2 cups (8 ounces) shredded
   mozzarella cheese
1½ cups freshly grated Parmesan
   cheese, divided
1½ teaspoons Italian seasoning
¼ teaspoon salt
1 (32-ounce) jar spaghetti sauce
Garnishes: fresh basil, freshly
   grated Parmesan cheese

Cook noodles according to package directions, and drain. Place noodles on layers of wax paper or plastic wrap.

Beat cream cheese at medium speed of an electric mixer until smooth. Stir in spinach, ricotta cheese, mozzarella cheese, 1 cup Parmesan cheese, Italian seasoning, and salt. Spread ½ cup cheese mixture evenly over each cooked noodle. Roll up, jellyroll fashion, starting at narrow end.

Pour spaghetti sauce into a lightly greased 13- x 9- x 2-inch baking dish. Cut lasagna rolls in half crosswise. Place rolls, cut sides down, over sauce in dish. Sprinkle top with remaining ½ cup Parmesan cheese.

Cover and bake at 350° for 25 minutes or until lasagna ruffles are thoroughly heated. Garnish, if desired. **Yield:** 6 to 10 servings.

EQUIPMENT NEEDED:
- Grater
- Dutch oven or large stockpot
- Electric mixer or wooden spoon
- 13- x 9- x 2-inch baking dish

Preparing rolls

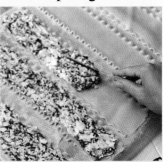

- Spread ½ cup cheese mixture evenly over each cooked noodle.

- Cut lasagna rolls in half crosswise, using a sharp chef's knife. Place rolls, cut sides down, over spaghetti sauce in dish.

Orzo and Olive Bake

EQUIPMENT NEEDED:
- Grater
- Large saucepan
- Large skillet
- 1½-quart casserole

What's orzo?
- Orzo is a tiny rice-shaped pasta that makes a great substitute for rice.

½ (16-ounce) package orzo, uncooked
1 large onion, chopped
1 cup chopped celery
2 tablespoons olive oil
1 tablespoon all-purpose flour
1 (16-ounce) can Italian-style tomatoes, drained
½ cup canned diluted chicken broth
1 tablespoon chopped fresh oregano or 1 teaspoon dried oregano
1 (4-ounce) can sliced ripe olives, drained
2 cups (8 ounces) shredded mozzarella cheese, divided
¾ teaspoon salt
¼ teaspoon ground red pepper

Cook orzo according to package directions; drain and set aside.

Cook onion and celery in hot oil in a large skillet over medium-high heat, stirring constantly, until tender. Add flour, stirring constantly until blended. Add tomatoes, broth, and oregano. Simmer 5 minutes. Stir in orzo, olives, 1 cup cheese, and salt. Spoon mixture into a greased 1½-quart casserole. Sprinkle with remaining 1 cup cheese and pepper. Bake, uncovered, at 400° for 20 minutes. **Yield:** 6 servings.

Pasta Primavera

1 **pound fresh asparagus**	1 **cup whipping cream**
2 **cups fresh broccoli flowerets**	½ **cup chicken broth**
1 **medium onion, chopped**	3 **green onions, chopped**
1 **large clove garlic, chopped**	2 **tablespoons chopped fresh basil**
1 **tablespoon olive oil**	½ **teaspoon salt**
1 **large carrot, scraped and**	8 **ounces linguine, uncooked**
diagonally sliced	½ **pound fresh mushrooms,**
1 **sweet red pepper, seeded and**	**sliced**
chopped	1 **cup freshly grated Parmesan**
1 **sweet yellow pepper, seeded**	**cheese**
and chopped	¼ **teaspoon ground pepper**

Snap off tough ends of asparagus. Remove scales with a vegetable peeler or knife, if desired. Cut asparagus diagonally into 1½-inch pieces. Place asparagus pieces and broccoli flowerets in a vegetable steamer over boiling water; cover and steam 6 minutes or until vegetables are crisp-tender. Remove from heat; set aside.

Cook onion and garlic in hot olive oil in a large skillet, stirring constantly, until tender. Add carrot and chopped peppers to onion mixture; cook, stirring constantly, until crisp-tender. Remove from heat; drain.

Combine whipping cream and next 4 ingredients in a medium skillet. Cook over medium-high heat 5 minutes, stirring occasionally.

Cook linguine according to package directions. Drain well; place in a large serving bowl. Add reserved vegetables, whipping cream mixture, and sliced mushrooms; toss gently. Sprinkle with Parmesan cheese and ground pepper; toss gently. Serve immediately. **Yield:** 8 servings.

EQUIPMENT NEEDED:
- Grater
- Vegetable peeler or knife
- Steaming basket
- Large skillet

Spring-style pasta
- The Italian term *primavera* means "spring-style," referring to the use of a variety of fresh vegetables. This pasta dish overflows with color and crunch.

Snapping asparagus

- Snap off the tough "woody" ends of fresh asparagus easily by bending the spears at the base.

Ravioli with Parmesan Sauce

3 tablespoons minced shallots or onion
3 tablespoons butter, melted
¾ pound fresh mushrooms, finely chopped
2 teaspoons minced garlic
¾ cup plus 2 tablespoons whipping cream, divided
½ cup diced cooked chicken
¼ cup finely chopped prosciutto
¾ teaspoon chopped fresh thyme
⅔ cup ricotta cheese
2 cups grated Parmesan cheese, divided

2 egg yolks, lightly beaten
3¼ cups plus 2 tablespoons all-purpose flour, divided
1½ teaspoons salt, divided
3 large eggs
1 tablespoon vegetable oil
1 to 2 tablespoons water
¼ cup plus 2 tablespoons butter
2½ cups milk
4 quarts water
½ cup butter, melted
Garnishes: chopped fresh parsley, chopped fresh thyme

Cook shallots in 3 tablespoons butter in a large skillet over medium-high heat, stirring constantly, until shallots are golden. Add mushrooms and minced garlic; cook, stirring constantly, until liquid evaporates. Add ¼ cup plus 2 tablespoons cream; cook over medium heat, stirring until liquid is absorbed. Stir in chicken, prosciutto, and ¾ teaspoon thyme; let cool. Stir in ricotta cheese, ¼ cup Parmesan cheese, and egg yolks; chill.

Combine 3 cups flour and 1 teaspoon salt; make a well in center. Combine 3 eggs, oil, and 1 tablespoon water; beat well. Add to flour mixture, stirring until blended. Add remaining 1 tablespoon water, if necessary. Turn dough out onto a floured surface, and knead until smooth and elastic. Cover; let rest 10 minutes.

Divide dough into fourths. Working with 1 portion at a time (keeping remaining portions covered) pass dough through pasta machine, starting at widest setting. Continue moving width gauge to narrower settings, passing dough through twice at each setting until dough is about 48 inches long, 6 inches wide, and 1/16 inch thick.

Place 1 strip of dough on a floured surface. Cut lengthwise into 2-inch-wide strips. Top with about 1½ teaspoons filling at 2-inch intervals. Moisten with water around filling; top with a second strip. Press with fingertips to seal. Cut between filling into 2-inch squares. Repeat procedure with remaining dough and filling. Let squares dry on a towel 1 hour, turning once.

Melt ¼ cup plus 2 tablespoons butter over low heat. Add remaining ¼ cup plus 2 tablespoons flour; stir until smooth. Cook, stirring constantly, 1 minute. Gradually add milk and remaining ½ cup cream; cook over medium heat, stirring constantly, until thickened and bubbly. Stir in 1½ cups Parmesan cheese; keep sauce warm.

Bring 4 quarts water and remaining ½ teaspoon salt to a boil in a Dutch oven; add half of ravioli at a time, and cook 10 to 12 minutes. Drain. Dip in ½ cup melted butter. Place in a single layer on baking sheets; sprinkle with remaining ¼ cup Parmesan cheese. Broil 5½ inches from heat 3 minutes (with electric oven door partially opened) or until golden. Serve ravioli with sauce. Garnish, if desired. **Yield:** 6 to 8 servings.

Fresh Tortellini au Gratin

½ pound mild Italian sausage
2 tablespoons chopped onion
1 (9-ounce) package fresh cheese-filled tortellini
3 cloves garlic, unpeeled
½ cup whipping cream
½ cup canned diluted chicken broth
½ cup freshly grated Parmesan cheese, divided
½ cup minced fresh parsley, divided

1½ tablespoons minced fresh basil
⅛ teaspoon pepper
1 (2-ounce) jar diced pimiento, drained
2 tablespoons fine, dry breadcrumbs
1½ tablespoons butter or margarine
Garnishes: sliced cherry tomatoes, fresh basil sprigs

Remove and discard casings from sausage. Cook sausage and onion in a skillet over medium heat until browned, stirring until meat crumbles. Drain.

Cook cheese tortellini according to package directions, adding unpeeled cloves of garlic to water. Drain well, reserving garlic. Set tortellini aside. Peel and crush garlic. Combine garlic and whipping cream in a medium bowl; beat with a wire whisk until blended. Add reserved sausage mixture, tortellini, chicken broth, ¼ cup plus 2 tablespoons Parmesan cheese, ¼ cup minced parsley, minced basil, pepper, and pimiento; stir gently.

Place tortellini mixture in a 1-quart baking dish. Combine breadcrumbs and remaining ¼ cup parsley; stir well. Sprinkle breadcrumb mixture over tortellini; dot with butter.

Bake at 325° for 40 minutes. Sprinkle remaining 2 tablespoons Parmesan cheese over breadcrumbs; bake 5 additional minutes or until lightly browned. Garnish, if desired. **Yield:** 4 servings.

Almond Rice

1¾ cups water
½ cup orange juice
½ teaspoon salt
1 cup long-grain rice, uncooked
2 tablespoons butter or
   margarine

2 tablespoons brown sugar
½ cup sliced natural almonds
1 teaspoon minced crystallized
   ginger
¼ teaspoon grated orange rind
Garnish: orange rind curls

EQUIPMENT NEEDED:
• Grater
• Saucepan
• Skillet

Keep rice covered
• To prevent gummy rice, keep it tightly covered while it cooks until all liquid has been absorbed.

Bring first 3 ingredients to a boil in a medium saucepan; gradually add rice, stirring constantly. Cover, reduce heat, and simmer 20 to 25 minutes or until rice is tender and liquid is absorbed.

Melt butter and brown sugar in a small skillet over medium heat. Add almonds and ginger; cook, stirring constantly, 2 minutes or until almonds are lightly browned. Add almond mixture and grated orange rind to rice, stirring gently. Garnish, if desired. **Yield:** 4 servings.

Black Beans and Yellow Rice

EQUIPMENT NEEDED:
- Dutch oven or large stockpot

1 large onion, chopped
1 medium-size green pepper, seeded and chopped
2 cloves garlic, minced
¼ cup olive oil
3 (15-ounce) cans black beans, drained
1 (14.5-ounce) can Cajun-style stewed tomatoes, undrained and chopped

1½ cups water
1 tablespoon red wine vinegar
1 teaspoon sugar
1 teaspoon pepper
½ teaspoon salt
1 (8-ounce) can tomato sauce
Hot cooked yellow rice
½ cup chopped green onions
Sour cream

Cook first 3 ingredients in hot oil in a Dutch oven over medium-high heat, stirring constantly, until vegetables are tender. Add beans and next 7 ingredients; bring mixture to a boil. Cover, reduce heat, and simmer 1 hour. Uncover and simmer 20 to 30 additional minutes, stirring occasionally.

Serve black bean mixture over hot cooked rice. Top each serving with green onions and a dollop of sour cream. **Yield:** 6 to 8 servings.

Cajun Jambalaya

★★★★★

EQUIPMENT NEEDED:
• 2-quart casserole
• Dutch oven or large
  stockpot

What's andouille?

• Andouille (an-DOO-ee) is
highly seasoned sausage used
in Cajun specialties. Cook the
spicy, smoked slices until
browned to draw out the rich
flavor.

¾ pound unpeeled large fresh
    shrimp
1½ teaspoons Cajun seasoning
3 skinned chicken breast halves
2 tablespoons butter or
    margarine, melted
1 tablespoon vegetable oil
½ pound andouille or other
    smoked sausage, sliced
1 large green pepper, seeded and
    chopped

1 medium onion, chopped
5 cloves garlic, minced
1 (28-ounce) can tomatoes,
    undrained and chopped
½ teaspoon salt
½ teaspoon pepper
¼ teaspoon Cajun seasoning
1 cup long-grain rice, uncooked
1½ cups water
Chopped green onions

Peel and devein shrimp; set aside.

Rub 1½ teaspoons Cajun seasoning over chicken. Place chicken in a lightly
greased 2-quart casserole; bake, uncovered, at 375° for 15 minutes. Drizzle
melted butter over chicken; bake 20 additional minutes or until tender. Let cool
to touch; bone and coarsely shred chicken.

Cook shrimp in hot oil in a Dutch oven over medium heat, stirring constantly,
until shrimp turn pink. Remove from Dutch oven; cover and set aside. Cook
sausage in Dutch oven until browned. Add green pepper, onion, and garlic to
Dutch oven. Cook, stirring constantly, 2 minutes. Add tomatoes and next 3
ingredients. Cover and simmer 20 minutes.

Add rice and water; cover and simmer 15 minutes. Uncover and cook 10 additional minutes or until liquid is absorbed. Stir in shrimp and shredded chicken;
cook until thoroughly heated. Spoon jambalaya into serving bowls; sprinkle
with chopped green onions. **Yield:** 6 servings.

Spanish Rice Cups

¼ cup finely chopped onion
¼ cup chopped green pepper
¼ cup chopped sweet red pepper
2 tablespoons chopped celery
1 clove garlic, crushed
2 tablespoons vegetable oil
1 (14½-ounce) can whole tomatoes, undrained
¾ cup long-grain rice, uncooked
¼ cup tomato sauce
1 bay leaf

Dash of ground red pepper
½ cup canned undiluted beef broth
1 teaspoon chili powder
½ teaspoon sugar
¼ teaspoon dried basil
¼ teaspoon dried oregano
1 green pepper
1 sweet red pepper
1 sweet yellow pepper

Cook first 5 ingredients in hot oil in a large skillet over medium-high heat, stirring constantly, until tender; drain.

Drain tomatoes, reserving liquid. Add enough water to tomato liquid to measure 1 cup. Chop tomatoes. Add tomato, tomato liquid, rice, and next 3 ingredients to vegetable mixture in skillet, stirring well. Bring mixture to a boil; cover, reduce heat, and simmer 10 minutes.

Add beef broth to rice mixture. Stir in chili powder and next 3 ingredients. Spoon rice mixture into a 1½-quart baking dish. Cover and bake at 350° for 35 minutes or until rice is tender and liquid is absorbed. Remove and discard bay leaf. Set rice mixture aside, and keep warm.

Cut whole peppers in half lengthwise, leaving stems intact. Remove and discard seeds. Cook peppers in a small amount of boiling water 3 to 4 minutes or until crisp-tender. Drain well. Spoon rice mixture evenly into each pepper half.
Yield: 6 servings.

Puffed Garlic-Cheese Grits

EQUIPMENT NEEDED:

- Grater
- Heavy saucepan
- Electric mixer
- 2-quart casserole

2 tablespoons butter or
   margarine
1 tablespoon plus 1 teaspoon
   minced garlic
4 cups water
¾ teaspoon salt
½ teaspoon black pepper
¾ teaspoon dry mustard
¼ teaspoon ground red pepper

1 cup regular grits, uncooked
1¼ cups (5 ounces) shredded
   sharp Cheddar cheese
½ cup (2 ounces) shredded
   mozzarella cheese
4 large eggs, separated
½ teaspoon cream of tartar
Dash of hot sauce
Garnish: paprika

Melt 2 tablespoons butter in a heavy saucepan over medium heat. Add garlic, and cook, stirring constantly, until golden. Add water, salt, and black pepper; bring to a boil, and stir in mustard and red pepper. Gradually stir in grits; return to a boil. Reduce heat to low; cover and cook 15 minutes or until liquid is absorbed, stirring occasionally. Remove from heat. Stir in cheeses and egg yolks. Transfer mixture to a large bowl; set aside.

  Beat egg whites and cream of tartar at high speed of an electric mixer just until foamy. Add hot sauce, and beat until stiff peaks form. Gently fold about one-third of beaten egg whites into grits mixture. Fold in remaining egg whites. Pour grits mixture into a greased shallow 2-quart casserole.

  Bake at 400° for 20 to 25 minutes or until grits are puffed and golden. Garnish, if desired. Serve immediately. **Yield:** 8 servings.

Tabbouleh

½ cup bulgur wheat
1 cup water
3 cups finely shredded lettuce
2 cups tightly packed, chopped
    fresh parsley (about 1½
    large bunches)
2 large tomatoes, seeded and
    finely chopped

1 small onion, minced
¼ cup chopped fresh mint
1 clove garlic, minced
¼ cup lemon juice
2 tablespoons olive oil
1 teaspoon salt
½ teaspoon pepper
Garnish: flowering kale

Combine bulgur and water in a medium bowl; cover and let stand 1 hour or until water is absorbed. Drain well in a strainer or small colander. Press excess water from bulgur, using a fork.

  Press lettuce and parsley between paper towels to remove excess moisture; toss together in a large bowl. Add bulgur, tomato, and next 3 ingredients; toss gently.

  Combine lemon juice and next 3 ingredients in a small bowl. Stir with a wire whisk, and pour dressing mixture over salad. Toss gently. Cover and chill 1 hour. Toss again just before serving. If desired, transfer Tabbouleh to a large salad bowl lined with kale. **Yield:** 6 cups.

★★★★★

EQUIPMENT NEEDED:
• Strainer or small colander
• Wire whisk

Make it a sandwich
• Tabbouleh makes a great filling for a pita pocket. Just add mayonnaise and a few tomato slices.

Draining bulgur

• Drain soaked bulgur wheat in a strainer or small colander. Press excess water from wheat, using a fork. This prevents salad from being soggy.

TANGY BARBECUE
SANDWICHES

FROSTED CRANBERRY-
CHERRY SALAD

Salads, Sandwiches & Soups

TOMATO SOUP WITH
HERBED CROUTONS

Four-Bean Marinated Salad

EQUIPMENT NEEDED:
- Saucepan
- Slotted spoon

1 (17-ounce) can lima beans, drained

1 (16-ounce) can cut green beans, drained

1 (16-ounce) can cut wax beans, drained

1 (16-ounce) can kidney beans, rinsed and drained

1 small green pepper, seeded and chopped

1 small onion, chopped

1 (2-ounce) jar diced pimiento, drained

¾ cup sugar

½ cup vegetable oil

½ cup white vinegar

½ teaspoon salt

½ teaspoon pepper

Combine first 7 ingredients in a large bowl; toss gently. Combine sugar and remaining 4 ingredients in a small saucepan; bring to a boil over low heat, stirring until sugar dissolves. Pour hot vinegar mixture over bean mixture; stir gently. Cover and chill at least 4 hours. Serve with a slotted spoon. **Yield:** 8 to 10 servings.

Caesar Salad

1 large clove garlic
2 tablespoons olive oil
1 teaspoon Worcestershire sauce
1 teaspoon Dijon mustard
1 teaspoon lemon juice
20 romaine lettuce leaves, torn
  (about 2 heads)

1 cup seasoned croutons
½ cup freshly grated Parmesan
  cheese
Salt and pepper to taste
Garnish: 1 (2-ounce) can anchovy
  fillets, drained

Crush garlic in a large salad bowl, using a garlic press. Add oil and next 3 ingredients; stir well, using a wire whisk. Add lettuce; toss to coat. Add croutons, cheese, salt, and pepper; toss again. Garnish, if desired. Serve immediately. **Yield:** 4 servings.

EQUIPMENT NEEDED:
• Large salad bowl
• Garlic press or mortar
  and pestle
• Wire whisk

Eggless Caesar
• Traditionally, Caesar Salad had a coddled (barely cooked) egg broken over the top. Because it's no longer safe to eat uncooked eggs, we've omitted the egg. Chop a hard-cooked egg for garnish, if you miss it.

Cornbread Salad

1 (8½-ounce) package corn muffin mix
2 cups packed torn romaine lettuce
2 stalks celery, chopped
1 large tomato, seeded and chopped
1 large green pepper, seeded and chopped
1 small purple onion, chopped
¼ cup olive oil
¼ cup lemon juice
1½ teaspoons dry mustard
½ teaspoon salt
½ teaspoon pepper
½ cup mayonnaise
½ cup chopped pecans, toasted
¼ cup chopped green onions

Bake muffin mix according to package directions in an 8-inch square pan. Let cool 10 minutes. Remove cornbread from pan; let cool, and cut into cubes. Place cubes on an ungreased baking sheet; bake at 250° for 1 hour.

Combine lettuce and next 4 ingredients; toss. Combine olive oil and next 4 ingredients. Pour olive oil mixture over salad. Stir in cornbread and mayonnaise. Sprinkle with pecans and green onions before serving. **Yield:** 8 servings.

BLT Chicken Salad

½ cup mayonnaise

¼ cup barbecue sauce

2 tablespoons grated onion

1 tablespoon lemon juice

½ teaspoon pepper

2 large tomatoes, chopped

8 cups torn leaf lettuce or iceberg lettuce

3 cups chopped cooked chicken

10 slices bacon, cooked and crumbled

2 hard-cooked eggs, sliced

Combine first 5 ingredients in a small bowl; stir well. Cover and chill dressing mixture thoroughly.

Gently press chopped tomato between several layers of paper towels to remove excess moisture. Arrange lettuce on individual salad plates; top each serving with tomato and chicken.

Just before serving, spoon dressing mixture over salads. Sprinkle salads with crumbled bacon, and top with egg slices. **Yield:** 4 servings.

EQUIPMENT NEEDED:

• Grater

• Egg slicer or knife

Slicing eggs

• Use an egg slicer to make slicing hard-cooked eggs a simple task.

Chicken Salad in Pastry

3½ cups chopped cooked chicken
1½ cups chopped celery
½ cup mayonnaise
¼ cup plus 1 tablespoon honey
    mustard
¼ cup finely chopped onion

1 teaspoon salt
¾ teaspoon cracked pepper
½ teaspoon dry mustard
¾ cup slivered almonds, toasted
Puff Pastry Ring
Curly leaf lettuce

Combine chicken and celery in a medium bowl. Combine mayonnaise and next 5 ingredients; stir well. Add to chicken mixture; toss gently. Stir in almonds. Split Puff Pastry Ring in half horizontally; remove and discard soft dough inside. Line bottom half of pastry ring with lettuce; top with chicken salad. Replace pastry ring top. **Yield:** 12 servings.

Puff Pastry Ring

1⅓ cups water
⅔ cup butter
1⅓ cups all-purpose flour

¼ teaspoon salt
¼ to ½ teaspoon celery seeds
6 large eggs

Trace or cut out a 9-inch circle on a piece of parchment paper. Turn paper over, and place on a greased baking sheet; set aside.

Combine water and butter in a medium saucepan; bring to a boil. Combine flour, salt, and celery seeds; stir well. Add to butter mixture, all at once, stirring vigorously over medium-high heat until mixture leaves sides of pan and forms a smooth ball. Remove from heat, and let cool 2 minutes.

Add eggs, one at a time, beating thoroughly with a wooden spoon after each addition; beat until dough is smooth. Spoon dough into a large pastry bag fitted with a large fluted tip. Working quickly, pipe dough into 12 rosettes on 9-inch circle on baking sheet.

Bake at 400° for 40 to 50 minutes or until puffed and golden. Let cool on a wire rack away from drafts. **Yield:** 12 servings.

EQUIPMENT NEEDED:
- Parchment paper
- Baking sheet
- Saucepan
- Wooden spoon
- Pastry bag and large fluted tip (optional)
- Wire cooling rack

Making pastry ring

• Pipe dough from a pastry bag for a fancy presentation. For an even easier method, simply spoon dough onto parchment paper.

German Potato Salad

16 new potatoes (about 1½ pounds)
6 slices bacon
½ cup chopped celery
1 tablespoon all-purpose flour
1 tablespoon sugar
2 teaspoons Dijon mustard
½ teaspoon salt

½ teaspoon celery seeds
Dash of ground white pepper
⅓ cup water
¼ cup white vinegar
½ cup chopped green onions
1 (2-ounce) jar sliced pimiento, drained
Garnish: celery leaves

EQUIPMENT NEEDED:
• Saucepan
• Large skillet

Cook potatoes in boiling salted water to cover 15 to 20 minutes or until potatoes are tender. Drain; let cool completely. Quarter potatoes; set aside.

Cook bacon in a large skillet until crisp. Remove bacon, reserving 3 tablespoons drippings in skillet. Discard remaining drippings. Crumble bacon, and set aside.

Cook celery in bacon drippings over medium-high heat, stirring constantly, until tender. Add flour and next 5 ingredients, stirring until smooth. Cook, stirring constantly, 1 minute. Gradually add water and vinegar; cook over medium heat, stirring constantly, until mixture is slightly thickened. Stir in potato, green onions, and pimiento. Cook just until thoroughly heated, stirring gently to coat. Transfer to a serving bowl. Sprinkle with bacon, and garnish, if desired. **Yield:** 6 to 8 servings.

Frosted Cranberry– Cherry Salad

★★★★★

EQUIPMENT NEEDED:

- Saucepan
- Food processor
- 10-cup mold
- Pastry brush

Grinding oranges

• Quarter and seed unpeeled oranges. Place in food processor, and process until ground.

3 (3-ounce) packages cherry-flavored gelatin	2 small oranges, unpeeled, quartered, and seeded
1 cup sugar	2 cups minced celery
2 cups boiling water	1 cup chopped pecans, toasted
1 (15¼-ounce) can crushed pineapple, undrained	1 cup fresh cranberries
2 tablespoons lemon juice	Light corn syrup
2 cups fresh cranberries	Additional sugar
	Curly leaf lettuce
	Garnish: lemon twists

Dissolve gelatin and 1 cup sugar in boiling water. Drain pineapple, reserving juice; set pineapple aside. Add enough water to pineapple juice to measure 1 cup. Add lemon juice. Add juice mixture to gelatin mixture, stirring well; chill until the consistency of unbeaten egg white.

Position knife blade in food processor bowl. Place 2 cups cranberries in processor bowl. Process until cranberries are ground. Remove cranberries. Repeat procedure with quartered oranges.

Add reserved pineapple, ground cranberries, orange, celery, and pecans to gelatin mixture; stir well. Pour salad mixture into a lightly oiled 10-cup mold. Cover and chill until firm.

Brush 1 cup cranberries with corn syrup, and coat with additional sugar. Let dry on wax paper. Unmold salad onto a lettuce-lined serving plate. Top with frosted cranberries. Garnish, if desired. **Yield:** 16 servings.

Lobster Salad

2½ quarts water
4 (8-ounce) fresh or frozen
    lobster tails, thawed, or 1
    pound seafood mix
½ pound fresh asparagus, cut
    into 1-inch pieces
1 cup chopped celery

½ cup mayonnaise
½ cup commercial French
    dressing
¼ teaspoon pepper
Bibb lettuce leaves
Garnish: tomato wedges

EQUIPMENT NEEDED:
• Large saucepan

Lobster alternative
• Seafood mix is an inexpensive substitute for lobster. It's a frozen blend of mild white fish fillets.

Bring water to a boil in a large saucepan; add lobster tails. Cover, reduce heat, and simmer 10 to 12 minutes. Drain. Rinse with cold water. Split and clean tails. Cut lobster meat into bite-size pieces.

Reserve 12 asparagus tips for garnish. Combine lobster, remaining asparagus, celery, and next 3 ingredients; stir gently to coat. Cover and chill 1 hour.

Serve chilled salad on lettuce leaves. Garnish with reserved asparagus tips and tomato, if desired. **Yield:** 4 servings.

Tangy Barbecue Sandwiches

EQUIPMENT NEEDED:
- Dutch oven
- Large saucepan

Beef works, too
- If you prefer beef over pork in your barbecue, substitute 1 (5- to 6-pound) beef rump roast in this recipe.

Shredding roast

- Shred tender cooked roast with two forks. Add Tangy Sauce, and simmer to blend the flavors.

1 (5- to 6-pound) Boston butt roast
6 whole cloves
2 medium onions, sliced
2 bay leaves
Tangy Sauce
Hamburger buns
Garnish: sliced dill pickles

Trim excess fat from roast. Place roast in a Dutch oven; add water to cover. Add cloves, onion, and bay leaves. Cover and cook over medium heat 2½ to 3 hours or until pork is tender. Drain meat, discarding onion, cloves, and bay leaves. Return meat to Dutch oven. Shred meat with two forks.

   Add 3 cups Tangy Sauce to shredded meat. Cook, uncovered, 20 minutes, stirring occasionally. Serve on buns with additional Tangy Sauce. Garnish, if desired. **Yield:** 12 servings.

Tangy Sauce

1 large onion, finely chopped
2 tablespoons butter or margarine, melted
2½ cups ketchup
1 cup white vinegar
1 cup water
⅔ cup firmly packed dark brown sugar
¼ cup Worcestershire sauce
2 tablespoons cracked pepper
2 tablespoons chili powder
1 tablespoon salt

Cook onion in butter in a large saucepan over medium heat until tender, stirring often. Add ketchup and remaining ingredients. Bring to a boil; cover, reduce heat, and simmer 30 minutes. **Yield:** 6 cups.

Calzones

1 package active dry yeast
1 cup warm water (105° to 115°)
3 to 3½ cups all-purpose flour, divided
¼ cup vegetable oil
1 teaspoon salt
1 pound ground pork sausage
½ cup chopped onion

2½ cups (10 ounces) shredded mozzarella cheese
1 teaspoon dried basil
1 teaspoon dried oregano
1 (6-ounce) can tomato paste
Olive oil
Marinara sauce
Garnish: grated Parmesan cheese

EQUIPMENT NEEDED:
• Grater
• Electric mixer
• Skillet
• Baking sheet
• Pastry brush or your fingers

Italian turnover
• A calzone is a large Italian turnover stuffed with pizza toppings. Smother it in your favorite brand of marinara sauce.

Dissolve yeast in warm water in a large bowl; let stand 5 minutes. Add 2 cups flour, vegetable oil, and salt; beat at medium speed of an electric mixer until blended. Stir in enough of remaining flour to make a stiff dough.

Turn dough out onto a lightly floured surface, and knead until smooth and elastic (about 5 minutes). Place dough in a well-greased bowl, turning to grease top. Cover and let rise in a warm place (85°), free from drafts, 1 hour or until doubled in bulk.

Cook sausage and onion in a skillet over medium heat until sausage is browned, stirring until meat crumbles; drain well. Combine sausage mixture, shredded cheese, and next 3 ingredients in a medium bowl; stir well.

Punch dough down; divide dough into 6 equal portions. Roll each portion to a 7-inch circle. Spoon ½ cup sausage mixture onto each circle; moisten edges of dough with water. Fold circles in half; press edges together with a fork dipped in flour. Transfer sandwiches to a lightly greased baking sheet. Flute edges, if desired. Brush dough gently with olive oil. Cover and let rise in a warm place, free from drafts, 30 minutes.

Make slits in top of dough to allow steam to escape. Bake at 400° for 25 minutes. Serve with marinara sauce. Garnish, if desired. **Yield:** 6 servings.

Meatball Subs

3 cloves garlic, minced
2 medium-size sweet red peppers, seeded and finely chopped
1 large green pepper, seeded and finely chopped
1 large onion, finely chopped
1 tablespoon vegetable oil
1 (28-ounce) can tomato puree
1½ pounds ground beef
½ cup Italian seasoned breadcrumbs

2 tablespoons chopped fresh parsley
2 teaspoons dried oregano
2 teaspoons dried thyme
1 teaspoon coarsely ground pepper
6 (6-inch) submarine rolls, split lengthwise and toasted
Grated Parmesan cheese
2 cups (8 ounces) shredded mozzarella cheese
Garnish: fresh thyme sprigs

Cook first 4 ingredients in hot oil in a Dutch oven over medium-high heat, stirring constantly, until tender. Add tomato puree; cover and simmer 30 minutes or until thickened.

Combine ground beef and next 5 ingredients in a large bowl, stirring well. Shape into 24 (1½-inch) meatballs. Broil meatballs on a rack in a broiler pan 5 minutes or until browned, turning once.

Add meatballs to tomato sauce, and simmer, uncovered, 2 to 3 minutes. Using a slotted spoon, place 4 meatballs on bottom half of each roll on a baking sheet. Spoon sauce over each sandwich. Sprinkle each with Parmesan cheese and ⅓ cup mozzarella cheese. Broil sandwiches 6 inches from heat (with electric oven door partially opened) until cheese melts. Cover each sandwich with top half of roll. Serve with remaining tomato sauce. Garnish, if desired. **Yield:** 6 servings.

Oyster Poor Boys

8 slices bacon
⅓ cup chopped onion
¼ cup chopped green pepper
¼ cup chopped celery
1 teaspoon garlic powder
¼ cup chopped fresh parsley
½ teaspoon seasoned salt
1 tomato, chopped and drained
⅓ cup mayonnaise
¼ teaspoon hot sauce
1 cup cracker meal

½ cup white cornmeal
¼ teaspoon seasoned salt
⅛ teaspoon pepper
2 (12-ounce) containers fresh
    Select oysters, drained
2 large eggs, lightly beaten
Vegetable oil
4 (6- to 7-inch) French bread
    loaves, sliced lengthwise and
    lightly toasted
Leaf lettuce

EQUIPMENT NEEDED:
- Large skillet
- Deep-fat fryer
- Tongs or long-handled
  spoon

Sizing up oysters
- Prepackaged oysters come
in two sizes, Standard and
Select. Select are the larger
ones.

Shrimp substitute
- To make Shrimp Poor Boys,
substitute 2 pounds unpeeled
large fresh shrimp, peeled and
deveined, for oysters.

Cook bacon in a large skillet until crisp; remove bacon, reserving 1 tablespoon drippings in skillet. Discard remaining drippings. Set bacon aside. Cook onion and next 3 ingredients in drippings over medium-high heat, stirring constantly, 2 to 3 minutes. Add parsley, ½ teaspoon seasoned salt, and tomato.

Remove tomato mixture from heat, and place in a bowl. Add mayonnaise and hot sauce, stirring well. Set mixture aside.

Combine cracker meal and next 3 ingredients in a medium bowl; stir well. Dip oysters in beaten eggs; dredge in cornmeal mixture. Fry oysters in deep hot oil (375°) for 1½ minutes or until golden, turning once. Drain on paper towels.

Spread mayonnaise mixture on bottom of each French bread loaf. Place lettuce, bacon, and oysters on bottom halves; replace tops. Serve remaining mayonnaise mixture with sandwiches. **Yield:** 4 servings.

Grilled Amberjack Sandwiches

EQUIPMENT NEEDED:
- Skillet
- Shallow container
- Grill

Serving seashells
- Serve tartar sauce in small seashells. Just be sure to wash them well.

¼ cup minced green onions
2 cloves garlic, minced
¼ cup olive oil
¼ cup dry white wine
2 tablespoons lemon juice
1 teaspoon cracked pepper
½ teaspoon salt

2 pounds amberjack fillets
4 kaiser rolls, split
Curly leaf lettuce
1 large tomato, sliced
1 purple onion, sliced
Tartar sauce

Cook green onions and garlic in hot olive oil in a skillet over medium-high heat, stirring constantly, until tender. Stir in wine and next 3 ingredients. Simmer 1 minute. Remove from heat.

Cut amberjack into 4 serving-size pieces. Place amberjack in a shallow container. Pour wine mixture over amberjack. Cover and marinate in refrigerator 1 hour, turning once.

Remove fillets from marinade, discarding marinade. Grill fillets, covered with grill lid, over medium coals (300° to 350°) 6 to 8 minutes on each side or until fish flakes when tested with a fork. To serve, butter and toast rolls. Top bottom half of each roll with lettuce, tomato, onion, tartar sauce, and a grilled fillet. Cover with tops of rolls. **Yield:** 4 servings.

Grilled Reubens

2 cups canned sauerkraut,
   drained
¾ teaspoon caraway seeds
Classic Thousand Island Dressing
12 slices rye bread without
   caraway seeds, divided

6 slices pumpernickel bread
12 (1-ounce) slices Swiss cheese
2 pounds corned beef, thinly
   sliced (about 48 slices)
Butter or margarine, softened
6 pimiento-stuffed olives

EQUIPMENT NEEDED:
• Griddle or skillet
• Wooden picks

Combine sauerkraut and caraway seeds; set aside. Spread 1⅓ cups Classic Thousand Island Dressing over 1 side of 6 slices rye and 6 slices pumpernickel bread. Place 1 slice cheese over dressing on each slice bread. Layer sauerkraut mixture and corned beef evenly over cheese slices. Stack to make 6 (2-layer) sandwiches. Spread remaining 6 rye bread slices with remaining dressing; invert on tops of sandwiches.

   Spread butter on outside of top slice of bread on each sandwich; invert sandwiches onto a hot griddle or skillet. Cook until bread is golden. Spread butter on ungrilled side of sandwiches; turn carefully, and cook until bread is golden and cheese is slightly melted. Secure sandwiches with wooden picks; top with olives. Serve warm. **Yield:** 6 servings.

Shortcut option
• Commercial dressing works well in this recipe if you don't have time to make our version.

Griddle cooking

• Turn sandwiches carefully on hot griddle, and continue cooking until cheese inside melts slightly.

Classic Thousand Island Dressing

1 cup mayonnaise
½ cup chili sauce
2 tablespoons salad olives
1 tablespoon chopped fresh
   parsley

1 tablespoon diced pimiento
2 teaspoons honey
½ teaspoon lemon juice
¼ teaspoon onion powder
12 capers

Combine mayonnaise and chili sauce; stir well. Add olives and remaining ingredients, stirring well. Cover and chill at least 1 hour. **Yield:** 1¾ cups.

Sourdough Sandwich Wheel

EQUIPMENT NEEDED:
- Electric or serrated knife
- Baking sheet

1 (9-inch) round loaf sourdough
   bread
¼ cup chopped ripe olives
4 (1-ounce) slices Cheddar cheese
1 medium-size purple onion,
   thinly sliced
2 tablespoons prepared
   horseradish
⅓ pound thinly sliced roast beef
4 (1-ounce) slices Monterey Jack
   cheese
3 tablespoons mayonnaise
1 medium tomato, thinly sliced
6 slices bacon, cooked and
   drained
3 tablespoons coarse-grained
   mustard

½ teaspoon poppy seeds
2 tablespoons minced onion
⅓ pound sliced cooked ham
4 (1-ounce) slices Swiss cheese
2 tablespoons butter or
   margarine, softened
⅓ pound thinly sliced cooked
   turkey
1 small green pepper, seeded and
   cut into rings
4 (1-ounce) slices colby cheese
¼ cup butter or margarine,
   softened
1 tablespoon sesame seeds,
   toasted
½ teaspoon onion salt

Slice bread horizontally into 6 equal layers, using an electric or serrated knife. Sprinkle bottom bread layer with olives, and top with Cheddar cheese, purple onion, and second bread layer.

Spread second bread layer with horseradish; top with roast beef, Monterey Jack cheese, and third bread layer. Spread third bread layer with mayonnaise; top with tomato, bacon, and fourth bread layer. Spread fourth bread layer with mustard; sprinkle with poppy seeds and minced onion. Top with ham, Swiss cheese, and fifth bread layer.

Spread fifth bread layer with 2 tablespoons softened butter; top with turkey, green pepper, colby cheese, and remaining bread layer.

Combine ¼ cup softened butter, sesame seeds, and onion salt; stir well. Spread mixture over top and sides of loaf. Wrap in heavy-duty aluminum foil; place on baking sheet. Bake at 400° for 30 minutes or until cheeses melt and sandwich is heated. Slice sandwich into wedges with an electric knife. **Yield:** 6 to 8 servings.

Muffulettas

EQUIPMENT NEEDED:
• Baking sheet

Serving option
• Omit the baking step, and serve Muffulettas at room temperature, if desired.

Olive salad

• Combine ingredients for the olive salad. It's packed with flavor and is what makes a Muffuletta unique.

2 (12-ounce) jars mixed pickled vegetables
½ cup pimiento-stuffed olive slices, coarsely chopped
3 tablespoons olive or vegetable oil
1 tablespoon minced garlic

1 (1-pound) round loaf Italian bread with sesame seeds
2 tablespoons olive oil
¼ pound thinly sliced salami
¼ pound thinly sliced pastrami
4 ounces thinly sliced mozzarella, provolone, or Swiss cheese

Drain mixed vegetables, reserving 1 tablespoon liquid. Finely chop vegetables. Combine vegetables, reserved liquid, olives, 3 tablespoons oil, and garlic; stir well, and set aside.

Slice bread in half horizontally. Drizzle 2 tablespoons olive oil over cut sides of loaf. Layer half of olive mixture, meats, and cheese alternately on bottom of loaf. Repeat with remaining ingredients. Top with remaining bread layer.

Slice sandwich into 4 wedges. Wrap sandwich in aluminum foil, and place on a baking sheet. Bake at 375° for 15 to 20 minutes or until cheese melts and sandwich is thoroughly heated. **Yield:** 4 servings.

Variation: To make individual sandwiches, substitute 4 (6-inch) French rolls for 1 pound round loaf. Slice rolls in half horizontally. Drizzle each roll with 1 tablespoon olive oil. Layer olive mixture, meats, and cheese alternately on bottom of each roll. Repeat with remaining ingredients. Cover with tops of rolls. Wrap each roll in aluminum foil, and place on a baking sheet. Bake at 375° for 10 to 15 minutes or until cheese melts and sandwiches are thoroughly heated.

Cream Cheese-Olive Club Sandwiches

2 (3-ounce) packages cream
   cheese, softened
2 tablespoons mayonnaise
2 teaspoons prepared
   horseradish
⅛ teaspoon pepper
Dash of garlic powder
¼ cup minced pimiento-stuffed
   olives
1 tablespoon grated onion

12 slices white or whole wheat
   bread, toasted
4 slices tomato
Salt and pepper to taste
8 (1-ounce) slices cooked turkey
4 (1-ounce) slices Swiss cheese
8 slices bacon, cooked and
   drained
Bibb lettuce leaves

EQUIPMENT NEEDED:
- Small grater
- Electric mixer
- Decorative or wooden picks

Combine first 5 ingredients in a small bowl; beat at medium speed of an electric mixer until smooth. Stir in olives and onion.

Spread 2 tablespoons cream cheese mixture on 1 side of each of 4 slices toast. Top each with 1 tomato slice, and sprinkle with salt and pepper to taste. Top tomato with 2 slices turkey and 1 slice Swiss cheese. Top cheese with 1 slice toast, 2 slices bacon, and lettuce.

Spread remaining 4 slices toast evenly with remaining cream cheese mixture. Place toast over lettuce, cream cheese mixture side down. Secure sandwiches with decorative picks; cut in half. **Yield:** 4 servings.

EQUIPMENT NEEDED:
- Skillet
- Dutch oven

Use the leaves, too!

- Finely chop celery leaves as well as stalks to flavor the soup. And save a few leaves for garnish.

Wild Rice Appetizer Soup

¾ cup butter or margarine, divided

1 large onion, finely chopped

3 cups finely chopped celery with leaves

½ pound fresh mushrooms, sliced

¼ cup all-purpose flour

1 teaspoon salt

½ teaspoon pepper

2½ cups milk

1½ cups half-and-half

1¾ cups cooked long-grain-and-wild rice mix

Garnish: celery leaves

Melt ½ cup butter in a skillet over medium heat; add onion, and cook, stirring constantly, until tender. Add chopped celery and mushrooms, and cook until tender. Set aside.

Melt remaining ¼ cup butter in a Dutch oven. Add flour, salt, and pepper; stir until smooth. Cook, stirring constantly, 1 minute. Gradually add milk and half-and-half; cook over medium heat, stirring constantly, until thickened. Stir in vegetables and rice; reduce heat to low, and simmer 15 minutes. Garnish, if desired. **Yield:** 8 cups.

Tomato Soup with Herbed Croutons

½ cup chopped onion
3 tablespoons butter or margarine, melted
3 tablespoons all-purpose flour
1 cup canned diluted chicken broth
1 (28-ounce) can Italian-style tomatoes, undrained
3 tablespoons tomato paste

1 tablespoon minced fresh parsley
1 tablespoon sugar
1 teaspoon salt
½ teaspoon dried basil
¼ teaspoon pepper
1 bay leaf
Herbed Croutons
Garnish: fresh basil sprigs

EQUIPMENT NEEDED:
- Dutch oven or large stockpot
- Electric blender
- Baking sheet

Cook onion in butter in a Dutch oven over medium-high heat, stirring constantly, 3 minutes or until tender. Reduce heat to low; add flour, stirring until smooth. Cook, stirring constantly, 1 minute. Gradually add broth; cook over medium heat, stirring constantly, until thickened and bubbly.

Add tomatoes and next 7 ingredients; stir well. Bring to a boil; cover, reduce heat, and simmer 30 minutes. Remove and discard bay leaf.

Spoon half of tomato mixture into container of an electric blender; cover and process until smooth. Repeat procedure with remaining tomato mixture. To serve, ladle soup into individual serving bowls. Top each serving with Herbed Croutons, and garnish, if desired. **Yield:** 3½ cups.

Herbed Croutons

2 slices white bread
1 tablespoon butter or margarine, melted

1 tablespoon grated Parmesan cheese
½ teaspoon dried basil

Trim and discard crusts from bread slices. Brush melted butter over bread; sprinkle with cheese and basil. Cut each slice into 4 squares; cut each square into 2 triangles. Place on an ungreased baking sheet; bake at 350° for 12 minutes or until croutons are dry and browned. **Yield:** 16 croutons.

Beer-Cheese-Potato Soup

2 medium baking potatoes
1 (12-ounce) can beer
1 cup canned diluted chicken broth
1 teaspoon Worcestershire sauce
½ cup half-and-half
¼ cup cornstarch
1 (16-ounce) jar process cheese spread

1 cup milk
¼ teaspoon ground red pepper
6 slices bacon, cooked and crumbled
½ cup (2 ounces) shredded sharp Cheddar cheese
Chopped fresh chives

Wash potatoes, and pat dry. Prick each potato several times with a fork. Bake at 400° for 1 hour or until done. Let cool completely; peel potatoes, and cut into chunks. Set aside.

Combine beer, broth, and Worcestershire sauce in a 3-quart saucepan. Cook over medium heat 4 to 6 minutes or until hot.

Combine half-and-half and cornstarch; stir well. Add cornstarch mixture, cheese spread, milk, and red pepper to beer mixture; stir well. Cook, stirring constantly, 4 minutes or until thickened and bubbly. Add reserved potato chunks; cook 2 minutes or just until thoroughly heated. To serve, ladle soup into individual serving bowls. Top each serving with crumbled bacon, shredded cheese, and chives. **Yield:** 8 cups.

Sausage, Bacon, and Bean Soup

¾ pound smoked sausage, cut
    into ¾-inch-thick slices
4 slices thick-sliced peppered
    bacon, cut into 1-inch pieces
2 medium onions, chopped
2 cloves garlic, minced
1 large green pepper, seeded and
    chopped
1 quart water
½ teaspoon seasoned salt
½ teaspoon dried thyme

½ teaspoon pepper
2 (15-ounce) cans kidney beans,
    drained
1 (28-ounce) can tomatoes,
    undrained and chopped
1 (8-ounce) can tomato sauce
1 bay leaf
2 cups peeled, coarsely chopped
    potato
¼ cup chopped fresh parsley

EQUIPMENT NEEDED:
- Large skillet
- Dutch oven or stockpot

Bacon options
- Thickly sliced peppered bacon is available at most grocers' meat counters. If you can't find it, substitute hickory-smoked prepacked bacon.

Cook sausage in a large skillet until browned; remove from heat, and set aside. Fry bacon in a Dutch oven until crisp. Remove bacon; set aside, reserving 1 tablespoon drippings in Dutch oven. Add onion, garlic, and green pepper to Dutch oven; cook, stirring constantly, 2 minutes. Add water and next 7 ingredients. Bring mixture to a boil; cover, reduce heat, and simmer 30 minutes. Add chopped potato; cover and simmer 30 additional minutes.

  Add sausage; cover and simmer 30 to 40 minutes. Remove bay leaf. Add bacon. Sprinkle soup with parsley before serving. **Yield:** 3½ quarts.

Steak Soup

2 tablespoons vegetable oil
2 pounds lean boneless round
    steak, cut into 1-inch pieces
Salt and freshly ground pepper
2 cloves garlic, minced
1 medium onion, chopped
5 cups water
½ cup Worcestershire sauce

1 teaspoon cracked pepper
½ teaspoon paprika
2½ cups medium egg noodles,
    uncooked (about 6 ounces)
2 cups sliced fresh mushrooms
2 cups (8 ounces) shredded
    Cheddar cheese

Heat oil in a Dutch oven over medium-high heat. Add meat, and sprinkle generously with salt and freshly ground pepper. Brown meat on all sides, stirring occasionally. Add garlic and onion; cook 2 minutes, stirring occasionally. Add water and next 3 ingredients. Bring to a boil; cover, reduce heat, and simmer 1 hour and 15 minutes.

  Stir in egg noodles and mushrooms. Bring to a boil; cover, reduce heat, and simmer 30 minutes or until meat is tender and noodles are cooked.

  Ladle soup into individual serving bowls; top each serving with cheese. **Yield:** about 7 cups.

Taco Soup

1½ pounds lean ground beef
2 large cloves garlic, minced
1 large onion, chopped
1 (1.25-ounce) package taco
    seasoning mix
½ cup water
3 tablespoons seeded, chopped
    jalapeño pepper
1 teaspoon ground cumin
1 teaspoon chili powder
2 (16-ounce) cans red kidney
    beans, drained

2 (4.5-ounce) cans chopped green
    chiles, undrained
1 (28-ounce) can whole tomatoes,
    undrained and chopped
1 (15-ounce) can tomato sauce
1 (10½-ounce) can beef broth,
    diluted
Finely shredded iceberg lettuce
Shredded Cheddar cheese
Chopped tomato
Corn chips

EQUIPMENT NEEDED:
• Grater
• Dutch oven or stockpot

Chip choices
• Try barbecue-flavored corn chips or scoop-size chips to top off this soup.

Cook first 3 ingredients in a Dutch oven until meat is browned and onion is tender, stirring until meat crumbles. Drain well; return to Dutch oven.

   Add taco seasoning mix and water to Dutch oven; stir well. Add chopped jalapeño and next 7 ingredients. Bring to a boil. Cover, reduce heat, and simmer 30 minutes, stirring occasionally. To serve, ladle soup into bowls. Top each serving with lettuce, cheese, chopped tomato, and corn chips. **Yield:** 15 cups.

Burgundy Beef Stew

EQUIPMENT NEEDED:
- Large shallow dish
- Dutch oven or stockpot

Marinating
- Marinating in a wine-vinegar mixture adds flavor and tenderizes the meat.

1 cup Burgundy or other dry red wine
2 tablespoons red wine vinegar
½ teaspoon pepper
¼ teaspoon ground allspice
2 cloves garlic, crushed
2 bay leaves
1 (8-ounce) can tomato sauce
2½ pounds beef for stewing, cut into 1-inch pieces
¼ cup olive oil
2 (10½-ounce) cans beef broth, undiluted

½ pound fresh mushrooms, halved
3 large carrots, scraped and diagonally sliced
1 (9-ounce) package frozen green beans
1 medium onion, coarsely chopped
2 tablespoons all-purpose flour
2 tablespoons water

Combine first 7 ingredients in a large shallow dish; stir well. Add meat; cover and marinate in refrigerator 8 hours.

Remove meat from marinade, reserving marinade. Remove and discard bay leaves; set marinade aside.

Heat oil in a Dutch oven over medium heat; add meat, and cook until browned on all sides. Drain and return to Dutch oven; add reserved marinade and broth. Bring to a boil; cover, reduce heat, and simmer 1½ hours. Add mushrooms and next 3 ingredients, stirring well; cover and cook 30 minutes or until vegetables are tender. Combine flour and water, stirring well. Stir flour mixture into stew, and cook until slightly thickened. **Yield:** 9 cups.

Tortilla-Corn Chowder

5 cups chicken broth
2 cloves garlic, minced
1 large onion, chopped
6 large ears fresh corn
4 (6-inch) corn tortillas, coarsely
   chopped
½ cup sour cream
2 to 3 tablespoons chopped fresh
   cilantro

¼ teaspoon salt
¼ teaspoon pepper
1 (4.5-ounce) can chopped green
   chiles, undrained
Garnishes: crushed tortilla chips,
   sour cream, fresh cilantro
   sprigs

EQUIPMENT NEEDED:
• Dutch oven or stockpot

Tortillas as a thickener

• Add tortillas to soup mixture. As tortillas simmer, they will soften and thicken the chowder.

Combine first 3 ingredients in a Dutch oven. Cut corn from cobs, scraping cobs well to remove all milk; add corn to Dutch oven. Stir in tortilla pieces. Cover and simmer over medium-low heat 1 hour and 15 minutes, stirring occasionally. Remove from heat.

  Stir in ½ cup sour cream and next 4 ingredients. Cook until heated. Ladle chowder into individual soup bowls. Garnish, if desired. **Yield:** 8 cups.

Variation: To make Cream of Corn Soup, transfer simmered corn mixture to container of an electric blender. Cover and process until smooth. Return mixture to Dutch oven. Stir in ½ cup sour cream and next 4 ingredients, and proceed as directed above.

HERBED CORN
ON THE COB

SPAGHETTI SQUASH ITALIANO

Vegetables

SOUTHERN FRIED
GREEN TOMATOES

Lemon-Buttered Asparagus

EQUIPMENT NEEDED:
- Vegetable peeler or knife
- Steamer basket

1 pound fresh asparagus spears
3 tablespoons butter or
   margarine, melted
3 tablespoons lemon juice

1 tablespoon grated Parmesan
   cheese
¼ teaspoon paprika
Garnish: lemon wedges

Snap off tough ends of asparagus. Remove scales with a vegetable peeler or knife, if desired. Place in a steamer basket over a small amount of boiling water. Cover and steam 4 to 6 minutes or until crisp-tender. Drain and arrange asparagus on a serving platter.

  Combine butter and lemon juice; stir well. Pour over asparagus. Combine Parmesan cheese and paprika; stir well. Sprinkle over asparagus. Garnish, if desired. **Yield:** 4 servings.

Note: If you prefer to microwave the asparagus, arrange asparagus in an 11- x 7- x 1½-inch baking dish with stem ends toward outside of dish; add ⅓ cup water. Cover with heavy-duty plastic wrap, and microwave at HIGH 6 to 7 minutes or until crisp-tender. Let stand, covered, 1 minute; drain. Arrange asparagus on serving platter. Proceed as directed above.

Hearty Baked Beans

1 pound dried navy beans
2 quarts water
1 small ham hock
1 bay leaf
¾ pound ground beef, cooked
2 cups ketchup
1 cup firmly packed brown sugar
3 tablespoons Worcestershire
   sauce

2 tablespoons molasses
1 tablespoon dry mustard
½ teaspoon ground ginger
1 large onion, chopped
1 small green pepper, seeded and
   chopped
1 (8-ounce) can tomato sauce

EQUIPMENT NEEDED:
• Dutch oven or stockpot
• 5-quart casserole

Softening beans

• Cover dried beans with water that comes 2 inches above beans, and let them soak overnight to rehydrate.

Sort and wash beans. Place in a Dutch oven. Cover with water 2 inches above beans; let soak overnight. Drain; return beans to Dutch oven. Add 2 quarts water, ham hock, and bay leaf. Bring to a boil; cover, reduce heat, and simmer 2 hours. Drain; reserve 1 cup liquid. Remove bay leaf. Remove ham from bone; chop. Add ham, beef, and remaining 9 ingredients to beans. Transfer to a greased 5-quart casserole; add reserved 1 cup liquid.

Cover and bake at 350° for 2 hours; stir occasionally. **Yield:** 10 servings.

Blue Cheese Green Beans

EQUIPMENT NEEDED:
- Electric blender
- Saucepan

1 ounce blue cheese, crumbled
3 tablespoons half-and-half
2 tablespoons white wine vinegar
1 tablespoon grated Parmesan cheese
½ teaspoon dried oregano
¼ teaspoon coarsely ground pepper
⅛ teaspoon sugar

¼ cup vegetable oil
1 pound fresh green beans
¼ teaspoon salt
Freshly ground pepper to taste
1 (2-ounce) jar sliced pimiento, drained
1 ounce blue cheese, crumbled
4 slices bacon, cooked and crumbled

Combine first 7 ingredients in container of an electric blender. Cover and process until smooth. With blender running, add oil in a slow, steady stream. Process just until blended; set dressing mixture aside.

Wash beans; trim ends, and remove strings. Cook beans in a small amount of boiling salted water 15 to 20 minutes or until tender; drain.

Arrange beans on a serving platter. Sprinkle with salt and pepper. Pour reserved dressing mixture over beans. Top with pimiento, 1 ounce crumbled blue cheese, and crumbled bacon. **Yield:** 4 servings.

Broccoli Stir-Fry

2 pounds fresh broccoli
2 tablespoons olive oil
1 tablespoon dark sesame oil
1 large sweet red pepper, seeded and cut lengthwise into strips
1 medium onion, cut into thin wedges
2 cloves garlic, minced
¼ cup soy sauce
¼ cup canned diluted beef or chicken broth

1½ tablespoons dark brown sugar
2 tablespoons red wine vinegar
1 tablespoon dark sesame oil
2 teaspoons cornstarch
1½ teaspoons minced fresh ginger
5 drops hot sauce
1 (8-ounce) can sliced water chestnuts, drained
¼ cup pine nuts, toasted

Trim off large leaves of broccoli, and remove tough ends of lower stalks. Wash broccoli, and coarsely chop stalks and flowerets.

Heat olive oil and 1 tablespoon dark sesame oil in a wok or a large nonstick skillet at medium-low (325°) for 2 minutes.

Add broccoli, red pepper, onion, and garlic; stir-fry 4 to 5 minutes or until broccoli is crisp-tender. Remove from wok. Combine soy sauce and next 7 ingredients; stir well. Add to wok; cook, stirring constantly, just until thickened. Return broccoli mixture to wok, and stir-fry just until thoroughly heated and coated. Stir in water chestnuts. Sprinkle with pine nuts before serving. Serve immediately. **Yield:** 6 to 8 servings.

EQUIPMENT NEEDED:
• Wok or large nonstick skillet
• Wooden spoon

The dark side of oil
• Dark sesame oil is made from toasted sesame seeds and has a full-bodied flavor. A little goes a long way. As a general rule, don't substitute it for other oils.

Add water chestnuts last

• Stir in water chestnuts just before serving to preserve their color; then sprinkle with pine nuts.

Brussels Sprouts with Walnuts

1½ pounds fresh brussels sprouts
½ cup olive oil
3 tablespoons red wine vinegar
2 tablespoons white wine Worcestershire sauce
1 tablespoon Dijon mustard
2 teaspoons sugar
½ teaspoon salt
½ teaspoon pepper
⅔ cup chopped walnuts, toasted
½ cup mandarin orange segments

Wash brussels sprouts; remove discolored leaves. Cut off stem ends, and cut a shallow X in bottom of each sprout. Place brussels sprouts in a saucepan; add water to cover. Bring to a boil; cover, reduce heat, and simmer 8 minutes or until tender. Drain. Transfer brussels sprouts to a serving bowl; keep warm.

Combine oil and next 6 ingredients in a saucepan. Cook over medium heat until thoroughly heated, stirring occasionally. Pour mixture over brussels sprouts. Add walnuts and orange segments; toss gently. Serve warm. **Yield:** 6 servings.

EQUIPMENT NEEDED:
- Pastry brush
- Grill

Choose your herbs
- Use any fresh herb combination in the butter mixture for this smoky grilled corn.

Husky wrapping

- Pull husks up over buttered corn; wrap in foil, and twist ends to seal for grilling. This lets the corn cook in its own juices and makes it taste extra fresh.

Herbed Corn on the Cob

4 ears fresh corn	1 tablespoon minced fresh
¼ cup butter or margarine, melted	parsley
	1 teaspoon minced fresh basil
2 tablespoons minced fresh chives	¼ teaspoon salt
	1 large clove garlic, crushed

Pull back husks from corn, leaving husks attached at base of cob; remove silks. Rinse corn; soak in water 20 minutes. Drain.

Combine butter and remaining 5 ingredients; stir well. Brush butter mixture over corn. Pull husks up over corn; wrap in heavy-duty aluminum foil, twisting foil at each end to seal. Place corn on rack of grill; cover and grill over medium-hot coals (350° to 400°) 35 to 40 minutes or until tender, turning occasionally. To serve, pull husks back, and tie in a knot. **Yield:** 4 servings.

Okra Fingers

20 small fresh okra pods
1 cup buttermilk
¾ cup all-purpose flour
1 teaspoon baking powder

½ teaspoon salt
¼ cup white cornmeal
⅛ teaspoon pepper
Vegetable oil

Wash okra; trim stems. Drain well, and place in a shallow container. Pour buttermilk over okra; set aside.

Combine flour and next 4 ingredients; stir well. Remove each okra pod from buttermilk, and roll in cornmeal mixture.

Pour oil to depth of 1 inch if using a deep skillet. Fry okra in hot oil (375°) for 3 to 5 minutes or until browned. Drain on paper towels. **Yield:** 4 servings.

EQUIPMENT NEEDED:
- Shallow container
- Deep-fat fryer or large deep skillet
- Tongs, large slotted spoon, or long-handled fork

Coating okra

- Pour buttermilk over okra to soak; then roll okra in corn-meal mixture.

Hearty Potato Casserole

8 medium baking potatoes
¼ cup plus 2 tablespoons butter or margarine, melted
¼ teaspoon paprika
¼ teaspoon pepper
2 tablespoons butter or margarine
2 tablespoons all-purpose flour
1½ cups milk
1 (8-ounce) carton sour cream
1 cup (4 ounces) shredded Gouda cheese
¼ teaspoon pepper
¾ cup diced cooked ham
½ cup chopped green onions
6 slices bacon, cooked and crumbled

Peel potatoes; cut crosswise into ¼-inch slices. Arrange potato slices in a lightly greased 3-quart shallow baking dish. Combine ¼ cup plus 2 tablespoons melted butter, paprika, and ¼ teaspoon pepper in a small bowl; stir well. Drizzle butter mixture over potato slices.

Cover and bake at 425° for 30 minutes. Uncover and bake 15 additional minutes or until potato is tender.

Melt 2 tablespoons butter in a heavy saucepan over low heat. Add flour, stirring until smooth. Cook, stirring constantly, 1 minute. Gradually add milk; cook over medium heat, stirring constantly, until mixture is thickened and bubbly. Add sour cream, Gouda cheese, and ¼ teaspoon pepper, stirring until cheese melts. Set cheese sauce aside, and keep warm.

Sprinkle ham and green onions over potato. Pour reserved cheese sauce over potato mixture. Cover; bake at 425° for 5 to 10 minutes or until bubbly. Sprinkle with bacon before serving. **Yield:** 8 to 10 servings.

Ultimate Stuffed Potatoes

4 large baking potatoes
¼ cup butter or margarine
¼ cup whipping cream
1 (8-ounce) carton sour cream
¾ cup (3 ounces) shredded sharp
    Cheddar cheese
½ cup chopped green onions

½ teaspoon garlic salt
¼ teaspoon pepper
1 ounce crumbled blue cheese
8 slices bacon, cooked and
    crumbled
Chopped fresh chives

EQUIPMENT NEEDED:
• Grater
• Potato masher
• Baking sheet

Wash potatoes, and pat dry; prick each potato several times with a fork. Bake at 400° for 1 hour or until done. Let cool to touch.

   Cut each potato in half lengthwise; scoop out pulp, leaving ¼-inch-thick shells. Place pulp in a large bowl. Add butter and whipping cream; mash until fluffy. Stir in sour cream and next 5 ingredients.

   Spoon potato mixture evenly into reserved shells. Place stuffed potatoes on a baking sheet. Bake, uncovered, at 400° for 10 minutes or until thoroughly heated. Sprinkle with bacon and chives. **Yield:** 8 servings.

Note: If you want to microwave the potatoes, prick them with a fork, and arrange them 1 inch apart in a circle on a layer of paper towels in microwave oven. Microwave, uncovered, at HIGH 18 to 20 minutes or until potatoes are tender, turning and rearranging potatoes after 8 minutes. Let cool to touch. Proceed as directed above.

Spaghetti Squash Italiano

1 (4-pound) spaghetti squash
⅓ cup water
1 tablespoon olive oil
2 cloves garlic, minced
1 small onion, chopped
2 large yellow squash, halved
    lengthwise and sliced
½ cup chopped sweet yellow
    pepper
1 medium tomato, seeded and
    chopped
1 (7-ounce) jar sun-dried
    tomatoes in oil, drained and
    cut into strips

1 tablespoon minced fresh basil
1 tablespoon minced fresh
    parsley
2 teaspoons minced fresh
    oregano
¼ teaspoon salt
⅛ teaspoon pepper
¼ cup grated Parmesan cheese,
    divided
Garnish: fresh basil sprigs

EQUIPMENT NEEDED:
- 13- x 9- x 2-inch baking
  dish
- Large skillet
- Grater

Microwave it
- A microwave cooks the large winter squash in a short amount of time.

Squash strands

- Remove spaghettilike strands to yield 4 cups squash for the filling.

Pierce spaghetti squash several times with a fork; place in a 13- x 9- x 2-inch baking dish. Microwave, uncovered, at HIGH 10 minutes. Cut in half lengthwise; remove and discard seeds.

Place spaghetti squash, cut side up, in baking dish; add water. Cover with heavy-duty plastic wrap, turning back one corner to vent. Microwave at HIGH 12 to 14 minutes or until tender, turning squash over every 5 minutes. Let stand 5 minutes. Drain; let cool.

Using a fork, remove spaghettilike strands to yield 4 cups, leaving two ¼-inch-thick shells. Place strands in a large bowl; set aside. Drain shells, cut sides down, on paper towels.

Combine olive oil, garlic, and onion in a large skillet. Cook over medium heat, stirring constantly, until onion is tender. Add yellow squash and yellow pepper; cook 3 to 4 minutes or until crisp-tender. Add onion mixture to reserved squash strands. Stir in chopped tomato and next 6 ingredients. Add 2 tablespoons Parmesan cheese; toss gently.

Spoon squash mixture into reserved squash shells. Place stuffed shells in baking dish, and microwave, uncovered, at HIGH 5 to 6 minutes or until thoroughly heated. (Or place baking dish in oven, and bake at 400° for 5 minutes.) Sprinkle with remaining 2 tablespoons Parmesan cheese. Garnish, if desired.
Yield: 6 to 8 servings.

Sausage-Stuffed Acorn Squash

EQUIPMENT NEEDED:
- Grater
- 13- x 9- x 2-inch baking dish
- Large skillet

Spicy or mild
- You choose whether to use spicy or mild sausage in this stuffing. Our test kitchen staff prefers spicy.

Scooping squash seeds

- Cut squash in half crosswise, and scoop out seeds.

3 medium acorn squash
1 pound ground pork sausage
3 cloves garlic, minced
1 medium onion, chopped
1 cup small-curd cottage cheese
1½ cups (6 ounces) shredded mozzarella cheese, divided
½ cup soft whole wheat breadcrumbs
¼ cup plus 2 tablespoons chopped fresh parsley, divided
1 tablespoon chopped fresh oregano or 1 teaspoon dried oregano
¼ teaspoon salt
¼ teaspoon ground red pepper
Paprika

Cut squash in half crosswise, and scoop out seeds. Place squash halves, cut sides down, in a 13- x 9- x 2-inch baking dish. (Cut bottom of each squash half to sit flat, if necessary.) Add hot water to a depth of ½ inch in dish. Cover and bake at 350° for 30 to 40 minutes or until tender. Drain squash on paper towels, cut sides down.

Combine sausage, garlic, and onion in a large skillet; cook over medium heat until sausage is browned and onion is tender, stirring until meat crumbles. Drain.

Combine sausage mixture, cottage cheese, ¾ cup mozzarella cheese, breadcrumbs, ¼ cup parsley, and next 3 ingredients; stir well. Spoon evenly into cooked squash halves. Return squash halves to baking dish. Combine remaining ¾ cup cheese and 2 tablespoons parsley; sprinkle over squash halves. Sprinkle with paprika.

Bake at 400° for 5 minutes or until thoroughly heated. **Yield:** 6 servings.

EQUIPMENT NEEDED:

- Grater
- Large saucepan
- Potato masher or fork
- 2-quart casserole

Mashing squash

- A potato masher makes an easy job of mashing cooked squash.

Country Squash Bake

10 large yellow squash, cut into pieces	1 cup soft whole wheat breadcrumbs
½ cup chopped onion	½ cup (2 ounces) shredded Cheddar cheese
1 (8-ounce) carton sour cream	¼ cup butter or margarine, melted
½ teaspoon salt	
½ teaspoon dried basil	
⅛ teaspoon ground red pepper	½ teaspoon paprika

Cook squash and onion in boiling water to cover 10 to 15 minutes or until tender. Drain well, and mash. Combine squash mixture, sour cream, and next 3 ingredients, stirring well. Spoon mixture into a greased 2-quart casserole.

Combine breadcrumbs and remaining 3 ingredients; toss well. Sprinkle over squash mixture.

Bake, uncovered, at 300° for 30 minutes or until thoroughly heated. **Yield:** 6 to 8 servings.

Easy Succotash

1 (10-ounce) package frozen lima beans

4 cups fresh corn (8 ears) or 1 (16-ounce) package frozen corn, thawed

1 small green pepper, seeded and finely chopped

1 small sweet red pepper, seeded and finely chopped

½ cup whipping cream

3 tablespoons butter or margarine, melted

½ teaspoon salt

¼ teaspoon pepper

EQUIPMENT NEEDED:
• Saucepan
• Large skillet

Native corn
• "Succotash" is a Native American name for boiled kernels of corn.

Cook lima beans in boiling salted water to cover 5 to 8 minutes or until beans are barely tender; drain. Transfer lima beans to a large skillet. Add corn and remaining ingredients. Cook over medium heat 10 to 15 minutes or until vegetables are tender, stirring occasionally. **Yield:** 6 to 8 servings.

Southern Fried Green Tomatoes

EQUIPMENT NEEDED:

• Large skillet

Coating tomatoes

• Our test kitchen prefers breading green tomatoes in fine white cornmeal. You can also coat them in cracker crumbs or breadcrumbs.

⅔ cup white cornmeal

¼ teaspoon salt

¼ teaspoon pepper

3 large green tomatoes, sliced

1 large egg, lightly beaten

¼ cup plus 2 tablespoons vegetable oil or olive oil, divided

Combine first 3 ingredients in a small bowl; stir well. Dip tomato slices in beaten egg; dredge in cornmeal mixture, coating well on both sides.

Heat 2 tablespoons oil in a large skillet over medium-high heat until hot. Add 1 layer of coated tomato slices, and fry 3 to 5 minutes or until browned, turning once. Remove tomato slices from skillet. Drain; set fried tomato slices aside, and keep warm. Repeat procedure twice with remaining oil and tomato slices. Serve immediately. **Yield:** 6 servings.

Tangy Broiled Tomatoes

4 large, firm tomatoes
Spicy brown mustard
½ teaspoon salt
¼ teaspoon black pepper
⅛ teaspoon ground red pepper

½ cup grated Parmesan cheese
½ cup Italian-seasoned
　 breadcrumbs
¼ cup plus 2 tablespoons butter
　 or margarine, melted

EQUIPMENT NEEDED:
• Grater
• Shallow baking dish

Cut tomatoes in half crosswise. Pat cut surfaces of tomatoes with paper towels to remove excess moisture. Spread about 2 teaspoons mustard over cut side of each tomato half.

　Combine salt and peppers in a small bowl; stir well. Sprinkle pepper mixture evenly over tops of tomato halves. Combine cheese, breadcrumbs, and butter; stir well. Spoon breadcrumb mixture evenly over each tomato half.

　Place tomatoes in a shallow baking dish. Bake at 350° for 5 to 6 minutes. Broil 4 inches from heat (with electric oven door partially opened) 30 seconds to 1 minute or until lightly browned. Serve immediately. **Yield:** 8 servings.

Basil-Zucchini Boats

EQUIPMENT NEEDED:
- Shallow baking dish
- Skillet
- Grater

2 medium zucchini (about 1 pound)

½ cup water

½ cup diced sweet red pepper

½ cup frozen tiny English peas, thawed

1 clove garlic, crushed

1 to 2 tablespoons olive oil

1 tablespoon chopped fresh basil

¼ cup grated Parmesan cheese

6 slices bacon, cooked and crumbled

Garnish: fresh basil sprigs

Cut each zucchini in half lengthwise. Scoop out pulp, leaving shells intact; chop pulp. Place zucchini shells, cut sides down, in a shallow baking dish. Add ½ cup water to baking dish.

Cover and bake at 350° for 8 minutes or until zucchini shells are crisp-tender. Drain; return shells to baking dish, cut side up.

Cook zucchini pulp, red pepper, peas, and garlic in olive oil in a skillet over medium-high heat just until red pepper is crisp-tender. Remove from heat. Stir in chopped fresh basil.

Spoon vegetable mixture evenly into zucchini shells. Sprinkle evenly with Parmesan cheese. Broil 5½ inches from heat (with electric oven door partially opened) 45 seconds to 1 minute or until thoroughly heated. Sprinkle with bacon. Garnish, if desired. Serve immediately. **Yield:** 4 servings.

METRIC EQUIVALENTS

The recipes that appear in this cookbook use the standard United States method for measuring liquid and dry or solid ingredients (teaspoons, tablespoons, and cups). The information in the following charts is provided to help cooks outside the U.S. successfully use these recipes. All equivalents are approximate.

Metric Equivalents for Different Types of Ingredients

A standard cup measure of a dry or solid ingredient will vary in weight depending on the type of ingredient. A standard cup of liquid is the same volume for any type of liquid. Use the following chart when converting standard cup measures to grams (weight) or milliliters (volume).

Standard Cup	Fine Powder (ex. flour)	Grain (ex. rice)	Granular (ex. sugar)	Liquid Solids (ex. butter)	Liquid (ex. milk)
1	140 g	150 g	190 g	200 g	240 ml
¾	105 g	113 g	143 g	150 g	180 ml
⅔	93 g	100 g	125 g	133 g	160 ml
½	70 g	75 g	95 g	100 g	120 ml
⅓	47 g	50 g	63 g	67 g	80 ml
¼	35 g	38 g	48 g	50 g	60 ml
⅛	18 g	19 g	24 g	25 g	30 ml

Useful Equivalents for Dry Ingredients by Weight

(To convert ounces to grams, multiply the number of ounces by 30.)

1 oz	=	1/16 lb	=	30 g
4 oz	=	¼ lb	=	120 g
8 oz	=	½ lb	=	240 g
12 oz	=	¾ lb	=	360 g
16 oz	=	1 lb	=	480 g

Useful Equivalents for Length

(To convert inches to centimeters, multiply the number of inches by 2.5.)

1 in				=	2.5 cm		
6 in	=	½ ft		=	15 cm		
12 in	=	1 ft		=	30 cm		
36 in	=	3 ft	=	1 yd	=	90 cm	
40 in				=	100 cm	=	1 m

Useful Equivalents for Liquid Ingredients by Volume

¼ tsp							=	1 ml	
½ tsp							=	2 ml	
1 tsp							=	5 ml	
3 tsp	=	1 tbls			=	½ fl oz	=	15 ml	
		2 tbls	=	⅛ cup	=	1 fl oz	=	30 ml	
		4 tbls	=	¼ cup	=	2 fl oz	=	60 ml	
		5⅓ tbls	=	⅓ cup	=	3 fl oz	=	80 ml	
		8 tbls	=	½ cup	=	4 fl oz	=	120 ml	
		10⅔ tbls	=	⅔ cup	=	5 fl oz	=	160 ml	
		12 tbls	=	¾ cup	=	6 fl oz	=	180 ml	
		16 tbls	=	1 cup	=	8 fl oz	=	240 ml	
		1 pt	=	2 cups	=	16 fl oz	=	480 ml	
		1 qt	=	4 cups	=	32 fl oz	=	960 ml	
						33 fl oz	=	1000 ml	= 1 l

Useful Equivalents for Cooking/Oven Temperatures

	Fahrenheit	Celcius	Gas Mark
Freeze Water	32° F	0° C	
Room Temperature	68° F	20° C	
Boil Water	212° F	100° C	
Bake	325° F	160° C	3
	350° F	180° C	4
	375° F	190° C	5
	400° F	200° C	6
	425° F	220° C	7
	450° F	230° C	8
Broil			Grill

Index